"STUCK IN THE MIDDLE"—THE MISUNDERSTOOD AGE

"STUCK IN THE MIDDLE"—THE MISUNDERSTOOD AGE

A HANDBOOK FOR CHRISTIAN EDUCATORS AND ESPECIALLY PARENTS

James DiVirgilio, BS, EdM, EdD, Temple University, Philadelphia, Pa., and Anne Adams, BS, Gettysburg College, Gettysburg, Pa., EdM, University of Maryland, College Park, Md.

VANTAGE PRESS
New York

Copyright © 1997 by James DiVirgilio, BS, EdM, EdD, Temple University,
Philadelphia, Pa., and Anne Adams, BS, Gettysburg College, Gettysburg,
Pa., EdM, University of Maryland, College Park, Md.

Published by Vantage Press, Inc.
516 West 34th Street, New York, New York 10001

Manufactured in the United States of America
ISBN: 0-533-12336-4

Library of Congress Catalog Card No.: 97-90264

0 9 8 7 6 5 4 3 2 1

The unhurried, unpredictable, misunderstood, changing, confused early adolescent

Contents

Introduction

Many parents and educators ask themselves, "Why have a Christian Middle School? Isn't secular education doing the job? It educated me!" Times have changed things in secular education, and we, who are of it, are in denial and don't want to admit it. Community beliefs and values were once derived from the Bible and were reflected in our schools. What a comfort. When I was in public schools sixty years ago, we had prayer, daily Bible readings in school, and a moral code based on biblical values. When my children were in public schools, twenty years ago, they had no daily Bible readings, no prayer, and unfortunately moral codes based on relativism, instead of biblical imperatives. Our public schools are not only void in the areas of prayer and Bible reading, but the whole environment seeps secular humanism, which influences everything that is taught.

The real problem is that society itself has changed expectations of the public school. No longer is the Judeo-Christian world view dominant. In its place came a man-centered secular humanistic world view, permeating everything. With this comes a different approach to the same subjects. Christian parents no longer can tolerate error-based teaching of subject content. There are common areas, to be sure, but these diminish daily. Even then, for early adolescents, teacher attitudes about things important to Christian parents do not reinforce a Christian value system. The same content can be differently inflected by the caustic, non-believing teacher. Some public school teachers are believers, thank goodness, but they still are limited in what they can do. This then is one of many differences between the public school years ago and now!

Another difference is in the way life is interpreted. The Christian school accepts and teaches the belief that man was created by God in his own image, and because he is a fallen creature, he cannot possess the wisdom of God, so his reasoning powers fail to be perfect. Yet modern philosophical thought, upon which our public schools are now based, assumes that man is capable of working out his own salvation, without God. What a fallacy!

This is man-centered secular humanism, which evolved over the years. Christians believe that man is more than a highly developed animal. Secular education, with its childish emphasis on the centrality of man, can only lead to a pervasive and pathological humanism, to a more corrupt world, where anything goes. How could it possibly lead to a nobler life, if man is all there is? This polarity between the Christian world view and the secular humanist world view indicates how wide the chasm is becoming. The Christian school not only accepts but strongly advocates the truth that God created something out of nothing. Things don't have to come from something with God.

Man is a being of accountability and responsibility for his own behavior. He has to answer to God for his own acts. God has provided him a way of salvation, but that does not depend on his goodness. The Bible says, "There is none that doeth good, no not one." A perfect secular humanistic environment will never make man fully perfect. The environment can modify a non-believer's behavior but not correct the heart. Man is too imperfect and is incapable of creating a perfect environment no matter how hard he tries. The Christian school will attempt to show man's need to seek God's help, and how to live accordingly. This development of conscience, based on absolutes of right and wrong, is the essence of Christian education.

For what good is man going to serve without understanding right and wrong?

Fortunately, public schools are not totally secular humanistic. There is still much good carried over from the past. Christian parents who have no alternative must become active on school boards and other decision-making bodies in order to preserve the good and recapture the Christian foundations of our society. The hope is still there. Christian teachers and administrators still abound in the public schools. They need your vocal support. All is not lost, if we work hard on the situation. Conditions vary from district to district. In promoting Christian schools, however, Christians have a grave responsibility to society not to desert the public school to the adversary. There is a need for Christians to be interested in and to support public education. We are our human brothers' keepers. Public schools will continue to enroll students from Christian families. Most of them have no choice but to enroll their children in public education. It's a real mission field for these parents.

It is the intention of the authors to provide ideas that will help Christian schools achieve the highest standard possible, without sacrificing Christian principles. It is the authors' further belief that a program advocated for a secular school can be even more successfully done in a Christian school. We can Christianize much of what we ignorantly reject. Therefore, in this book, no program has been automatically eliminated. The application of the growth level facts are similar in both secular and Christian children. Some of the extremes may be different. Much information is available about the development of children and their need for the specific middle level education advocated in this book.

The authors believe that a misguided, non-professionally behaved Christian teacher can set up a poor classroom in a Christian school in which early adolescents will misbehave. Early adolescents don't need much prodding to misbehave;

even when they are redeemed, they have problems. Teacher understanding, of growth and development, is imperative. This book was written with the recognition of man's original sinful condition, and also that man needs to learn to refine his actions. Good ethics are important and should permeate all programs of a Christian school.

The following was taken from the Chapelgate Christian Handbook and points out the value of a truly Christian school.

> The purpose of the school is both to provide a quality academic program integrated with a Christian world view of God and His world; and also to equip young people to serve the Lord effectively in church and in the community at large.
>
> There is an important difference between the Christian and the non-Christian view-point on any given academic subject. No subject can be fully understood or properly taught if its relationship to the Creator is ignored or denied. Only the scriptural approach to education can be God-honoring for Christian parents and their children.

The authors further believe that this book presents a workable process for Christian schools, that affirms and accepts the best knowledge known to man synchronized with sound Christian beliefs, and encourages schools to use it! In other words let's not throw the baby out with the bath water in our suspicion of public education.

A successful Christian school will have as its goal to educate students so they are encouraged to exhibit the fruit of the Spirit. As explained in Galatians 5:22–23: "But the fruit of the Spirit is love, joy, peace, longsuffering, gentleness, goodness, faith, meekness, temperance, . . . "(KJ). What could be nobler?

The answer to the original question, "Why have a Christian middle school?" becomes clearer as this introduction develops.

The need for Christian elementary schools is clear to many Christian parents. But why a middle school? After reading this introduction, the reader's doubt should be diminished. There should be no doubt that this impressionable age needs Christian guidance. At the risk of repetition, the authors will recap the situation. Don't we believe that if parents can teach their children values when they are young enough, middle school isn't needed? The Bible says, "Train up a child in the way he should go, and when he is old, he will not turn from it" (Prov. 22:6, NIV).

But it must be remembered that this verse does not state our responsibility for such training ends at ten or even eleven years of age! It stresses the need for a good start. The training of a child is a continuing responsibility that goes on for a lifetime. The middle school age is very important for the development of those lifetime values. The contention of this book is that the early adolescent child is impressionable spiritually, mentally, physically, and emotionally. Not only is it essential to have early adolescents under influences consistent with their Christian upbringing, but it is also imperative that they have a specific, middle level educational blueprint, designed for this unique age.

This same understanding spurred the middle school concept in secular education. The secular middle school came into being because there was discovered to be a need to create schooling specifically structured for early adolescents. The junior high was too secondary (adolescent) in its orientation. The mere presence of older adolescents caused it to adopt practices that were not suitable to the majority of the student body. The early adolescent did not perform well in a school that was a clone of the high school. Youth leaders in our churches need to be cognizant of this. Their middle school and high school programs ought to be significantly different.

The middle school concept is based on the understanding

that early adolescents are vastly different from their counter-parts in either elementary or high school. Educators and parents need to be cautioned that merely creating a school made up of grades 6 to 8 by no means makes it a true middle school. It's a good start, but there is more to it than that. A true middle school takes into consideration the developmental changes taking place in early adolescents, and provides staff, curriculum, and atmosphere designed for them. See the evaluation instrument in the last chapter of this book to determine how much of the middle school concept your school is fulfilling. Though not scientifically developed, it is a good guideline. Use it.

This book emphasizes the need to consider the spiritual, mental, physical, and emotional needs of the early adolescent, and for the design of a school that is sensitive to those needs. It will further use this information to justify and shape the design of the curriculum, teaching methods, home room activities, schedule, administrative actions, and parental responsibilities. We hope that this book broadens your knowledge of middle school education and helps you produce outstanding Christian middle schools. We dream that the book stimulates the execution of a creative school environment in which the students will maximize their potential. The best way to serve the Lord, is to help nurture spiritual, mental, physical, and emotional health of young people at this vital age in their lives. God be praised!

A Brief Abstract

This book was developed by leading educators in the original middle school movement. The authors firmly believe that the middle school movement with its emphasis on the growth and development of early adolescents is sound and constantly needs re-emphasis. *"Stuck in the Middle"—the Misunderstood Age,* appropriately emphasizes the position in which the early adolescent (10 to 14 years old) finds himself. The book makes a strong appeal that the physical, emotional, mental, and spiritual development of these children is crucial to normal growth. By reading this book parents, school board members, teachers, youth leaders, administrators, and even secular educators will derive much from it. As well as the strong emphasis on these developmental levels, the book impacts on teaching methods, curriculum, testing, assignments, report cards, discipline, and interest areas. All with the Christian perspective in mind.

The merits of this book should not be underestimated by anyone responsible for this age level. The authors believe that early adolescents need a supportive adult world that isn't rushing them beyond their age.

The book is purposely written in a non-jargon language easily understood. The simplicity of the language is meant to promote good communications. It is intended to be informative. The authors depend on their own real-live experiences with middle schools.

"STUCK IN THE MIDDLE"—THE MISUNDERSTOOD AGE

1

The Unpredictable, Inconsistent Student

Welcome to the world of middle school, a complex world with students who have conflicting needs. Often misunderstood, this species is very special. They need a whole level of education devoted just to them. People often ask, "Why can't sixth graders stay in elementary school? Why can't ninth graders stay with seventh and eighth graders? Why can't seventh and eighth graders be in a high school?" The purpose of this book is to point out the need for middle level professionals to develop education that is suited to the 10 to 14 year old, (grades 6 through 8), whom I will call the early adolescent. This age has its very own maturation problems.

When middle schools first started, teachers remembered their experience with junior high students and said, "That's the last place we want to teach." It didn't take long for teachers to discover that these same early adolescents were a pleasure to teach in their own environment, where there was an understanding of their physical, emotional, and social growth. Middle school then became the preferred level of many teachers.

Back in the sixties, it was concluded that children were developing more quickly than in previous generations, and needed an education level more suited to their rapidly changing bodies. One conclusion was that sixth graders needed something more mature than what the normal elementary school could provide. Some girls started menarche, the menstruating period, as early as fourth grade. These children were arriving at puberty one and half years earlier than previous generations. Most seventh and eighth graders are also going through this stage. Grades six, seven, and eight make a natural set. Some middle schools include the fifth grade, but only about 15 percent of fifth graders have arrived at puberty, so they can remain in elementary school, which is suited to the needs of the majority. This move of the sixth grade is not an attempt to push what today is called, "the hurried child syndrome." In fact it is just the opposite. It is an attempt to put most pubescent children together in one school, which is alerted to their needs. The intention is to take them as they are, and not to complicate their lives during this impressionable age. They have enough problems of their own.

Meanwhile the ninth graders were maturing faster too. They were arriving at adolescence earlier than previous generations. Their needs would be better served in a school with other adolescents. They often were in a junior high that in essence was two schools, one for seventh and eighth graders, and one for ninth graders with its Carnegie Units and college preparation courses. Also, they were social misfits. The older ninth grade students and junior highs became too sophisticated for the rest of the student body. A better environment for the 10 to 14-year-old student was needed. Thus the middle school. Without change the early adolescent probably will have difficulty developing normally.

In more than twenty-five years of working with middle school administrators, teachers, students, and parents, I frequently have been convinced that middle school-aged students need a separate school. In a series of teacher workshops, which I conducted over the years, I asked teachers in public, private, secular, and Christian schools to list the characteristics of the students they taught daily in middle school. The responses were similar no matter whether what the students attended was public, secular, private or Christian school. It is interesting to note that many of the characteristics are opposites, even for the same child, revealing the dilemma through which the early adolescent is passing. Professionals who are responsible for this age level would do well to study these characteristics and determine what methods, discipline, and environment would serve best, and also figure out what would serve worse. Once again I would like to remind you to get a feel for the conflicting behavior these children exhibit. Christian schoolchildren go through the same growth problems as non-Christians. Here is the list of student characteristics. Study it.

energetic/lazy
peer group oriented/please adults
parent stupidity/other significant
adult
impulsive
talkative/inward
restless—drums on desk
wants attention
playful/too serious
caring, favors underdog
noisy
curious
honest/fair minded
self-centered/hyperactive
changeable
moody/happy
shy/bold
inconsistent
mannerly/crude

What an imposing description of the middle school children composed by teachers who teach in middle school. There is a definite need for a proper program with classroom organization, clear teaching methods, reinforcing adults, and an understanding discipline. With a staff that understands and accepts these characteristics and properly responds to them, problems are minimal. In other words, when administrators and teachers understand and respond well to the struggles of the early adolescent, their duties become pleasant.

Review the characteristics of middle level students, and notice they really are children. At best, they are just emerging in social situations and lack polish. Consequently, their oral responses may be gruff. They experiment with sounding adult and they do it very poorly. We can help them or we can unintentionally place obstacles in their paths. They repeatedly respond in immature ways. They badly need to refine their social skills. In many instances they are behind a facade and are actually very scared. A keen observer can notice evidence of this in the vast difference in physical sizes and also in the varied interests. The variety in the rate of physical and mental change is as pronounced as the variety in size. Keep in mind a student with a large overgrown body may be undergrown in emotional, mental, and even in maturation. These categories do not necessarily grow in harmony with each other. The less visible changes happen on the inside at many different paces. It is possible for the adult to be caught unawares, and, because of an overgrown and well-developed body, to expect a mature reaction. But the reaction may still be very immature. Though I risk boring you, let me stress the importance of what has been written above by repeating some of the typical characteristics of early adolescent children ages 10 to 14.

Even though they seemingly openly reject adults, they need adult supervision and guidance. I cannot overemphasize the importance of adults in their lives. The Scriptures point this out when writing about the duty of a father. I believe this is good advice for other significant adults too. Ephesians 6:4: "And, ye fathers, provoke not your children to wrath: but bring them up in the nurture and admonition of the Lord" (KJ). Also the Scriptures say, "Fathers, do not embitter your children, or they will become discouraged" (Col. 3:21, KJ).

Children this age already are confused, and are not well equipped to help each other. They are quick to make fun of the weakest one who is different. In fact, this fair-minded group can be cruel at times. This cruelty can be demonstrated even among best friends.

First, all who work with this age notice the obvious physical growth, rapid, slow, or in-between. Parents can recognize changes taking place in weight, voice, height, physical coordination, energy, and bravado. The early adolescent is very sensitive to these changes. An insensitive adult who makes fun of a male's changing voice or his clumsiness is not what the early adolescent needs. They don't know how to handle peer ridicule either, yet they dish it out. They need assurance from parents, teachers, and others, even when they respond inappreciatively. Such changes are embarrassing to the students who have them, and to the students who don't. Imagine, if you suddenly had body hair and others didn't, or your voice cracked earlier than those of your peers. How can students grow well emotionally, if these worries are aggravated by teachers and other adults?

In addition there are spurts of energy followed by fatigue, making students appear lazy. Take as an example, slumping in a chair. How should the teacher handle this? By yelling, "I've told you before and I'm not telling you again. Do you hear me?" By lecturing on disrespect? By making an example of the student? By showing him who is boss? No! The authors have observed an effective teacher who knew how to take advantage of this teachable moment and used it for class learning. The teacher calmly walked over to the student, put a hand on his shoulder, and quietly, unembarrassingly, privately said, "It's a good thing I know you and that you aren't a disrespectful student. You need to sit up." The situation was corrected without an attempt to embarrass him.

If the student persisted, the teacher might go over to the student and schedule a time of meaningful detention first and more detention or even a parent conference later. But first students should be given a chance to respond positively. The teacher knew students would slump, because of the tremendous bodily changes that were happening developmentally. In time such a student will learn how to handle this problem. This teacher held the student accountable in a non-threatening way. It is a mistake to excuse misbehavior; it must be handled.

Another common irritating example for students at this age level is the constant drumming of fingers. This can drive the teacher to distraction. Handle it sensitively. The student may not be aware that it is being done. Allow the student to preserve self-respect. The teacher should apply strong, firm, understanding discipline.

Another common characteristic of this age is awkwardness. They trip over their own feet. Often their arms and hands are not synchronized with their feet. Sometimes they grope for proper words to say and often cannot find any. They are conscious of this and extremely uneasy with it. They need constant assurance that, given time, they will cope with these situations easily. Nervousness and tenseness only make matters worse.

Another common characteristic that gives them difficulty is the growth of the intellectual thought processes. Organized thought process is not their strength. The mind is having difficulty working in unison, just like the body. Sometimes one part of the mind matures in function before the rest. In his study on brain periodization, Dr. Connie Toepfler discovered that in most early adolescents at some time in the developmental period, the brain takes a rest in the growth pattern. This is more noticeable in some children than in others. It also is not in lockstep. Not every member of one class is at the same developmental level. But teachers must realize this because it reveals the student's ability to handle abstract subjects.

For example, many students take Algebra I prematurely. Then their next year's mathematics teacher finds that even students who make an "A" may not be able to remember and synthesize on the basis of what they learned the previous year. It is just as if they never took Algebra I. Abstract learning in depth depends on human growth and development in all areas, especially the brain. All I'm saying is proceed with caution. It is better for a student to wait until he matures than to be pushed into advanced courses before maturation takes place. We must tie learning to human growth and development. It is fine to push advanced courses that are practical and not full of abstractions. Understand!

We're living in a day when parents and even educators are pushing children into courses for which they haven't lived long enough to acquire sufficient background to understand a subject's intricacies. How much better it would be to develop them into scholars instead of regurgitators.

Another common characteristic is a short memory span. Parents need to recognize this too. Middle school teachers who are aware of this will schedule frequent checkups, on class time, when assigning long-term projects. This prevents tension and conflict because the disorganized early adolescent didn't plan time wisely. It also avoids the submitting of an inferior, hurried project. Set reasonable limits and hold students to them. Given time, they will grow into being able to excel in long-term projects. Right now they are not there yet, no matter how hard the teacher tries to help.

Remember, in all of this, there are extreme individual differences. There are too many growth complications taking place in 10 to 14-year-old students at this time for teachers to fully understand the varied student reactions. The consequences are frequent personal confrontations with students. I'm not making excuses for early adolescents. I am saying that, if understood and properly taught, they will enthusiastically support the learning process, and not build up a rebellious attitude that will stay with them for the rest of their school life.

Teachers in middle schools should keep projects challenging, interesting, and short. Projects should be designed not to encourage plagiarism. Show them what plagiarism is, and what it is not.

Another common characteristic of an emerging 10 to 14-year-old is classroom boredom. A common complaint is, "The teacher does the same thing every day." Routine unstimulating teachers blame the subject for that. Creative teachers know that early adolescents respond well to an active classroom, with periodic movement. With limited attention spans, a change of pace is needed. Early adolescents shouldn't be expected to sit still and be quiet every period. Planned method changes are very effective. However, the students must not be able to manipulate teachers. They must realize that the teachers planned the changes. When procedures are changed by teachers in a classroom, the students must not be suddenly released, but must be done in an orderly manner and teacher directed. They need to be challenged to know when to move, where to move, how to comport themselves, and the teacher's expectations of the process. Having things done decently and orderly adds to their sense of security, and adds to their emotional health.

Some would say we are spoon-feeding the students. I say we are intelligently leading the students from one age level to another in a wholesome way. Expectations of the students will expand as they grow. Good teaching leads to healthy growth. Relationships between children and children, and between adults and children are also needed. Preadolescent children love to be involved in the learning process; let's involve them. All learners appreciate involvement. The major difference is that the 10 to 14-year-old students' reaction to poor teaching is negative and their feelings are quickly shown. On the other hand, they can be very enjoyable and responsive in a well-run class no matter how difficult the subject matter. Classroom procedures and the classroom atmosphere are very important to them. Even an attractive room, full of student work, contributes to a good middle school environment, and encourages enthusiastic participation.

The sixth characteristic is emotion or temperament. Emotional outbursts that are out of control need not happen. With emotional growth students experience frustration, calmness, despair, sadness, happiness, and more. Their environment must encourage them to cope with their own problems and help others with theirs. Clumsy as they may be at school, they need constant adult supervision, and understanding teachers who are orderly, encouraging, and humorous and who spell out limits necessary for good healthy emotional growth.

These are but a few of the ingredients. We must not forget teachers need good, healthy mental hygiene themselves. The teachers must have it all together for themselves if they are to help these children grow into healthy adults. Students need to be free from complications caused by well-intended teachers who are unfamiliar with the process of human development. Again I state that students respond well to empathetic, firm, organized teachers who are confident, knowledgeable of their subject, and above all comfortable with their pupils.

We can't put middle school-aged children into a cocoon and wait for them to grow into teenage adolescents. The middle school must be their cocoon. A good middle school experience will result in healthy teenage adolescents. What a glorious opportunity for those involved in middle school.

Primary influences affecting children 10 to 14 are community and church youth leaders. They advocate what they think are reasonable programs. They would do well to familiarize themselves with the above characteristics, if they want to minimize frustrations. Many times they advocate programs that are inappropriate for middle school age children. Often from sympathy or ignorance, they will plan an overly sophisticated activity better suited for older children. Naturally early adolescents gravitate toward sophisticated activity, because they look up to older students who are ready for such. Early adolescents can't wait to be older. Even if they can't yet handle it for long, they think of it as being "cool." But if middle school youngsters are to go camping, then plans for accommodations, activities, and schedule must not be just imitations of those appropriate for adolescents.

Community conflicts are prevalent, too. Community leaders and church leaders would do well to get together with middle school professionals and develop guidelines for this age level. In this way, their goals will better promote the growth of these youngsters. Church and community leaders need advice on how to foster good growth.

Sometimes high schools and older youth groups have functions to which middle school youngsters are invited. They attend, even when they know little about the event. Appropriate event or not, they will be there. Sometimes they are invited to swell attendance or to sell tickets. But at whose expense? If they share the adolescent activity, most of them won't know how to absorb everything properly. Then they won't want to do those activities when they do reach the right age. They lose interest because it is something they have already done. This was one problem with the junior high. Things became "old hat" by high school. The same can happen with young people's groups at church. What a bummer! So when youth groups or community groups sponsor activities that really aren't suited for younger youth, we should insist that they have something separate and more appropriate for the younger middle level youth.

The last influence I will discuss is in the upcoming communications area. In this technological world, it is very difficult to control the negative influences on these immature minds. They will be exposed to influences they are not ready to process. Television alone, with its multiple channels, will have programs that would make adults blush. Then think of the possibilities for smut, on "networks." This makes the Christian school that much more imperative. We need to work on character and standards, building up independence so that peer attitudes that reinforce goodness and high standards will assist middle level students resist these temptations. With the arrival of the limitless information of the Internet, it will become even more important to develop character in our students. Christian schools need to prepare students to make wise choices. Our students need to learn decision-making for times when the decisions cannot be monitored by an adult. We need to be vigilant and to watch for porn but not overreact when it happens. We should model behavior even by our reactions to bad influences.

Even comic books, which used to be innocent reading, are getting sordid. It is virtually impossible for the parent or other significant adult to keep up to date on the latest changes. Certainly, these students need a combination of adult no-no's, and their own sound decision-making, which the schools, along with the parents, can help. Expect some inconsistencies. We must be kind, firm, loving, and patient. Be assured it will work out.

Remember students need differing treatment. Yes, there will be times of agonizing and soul searching. Whether you are a teacher, a parent, or some other significant adult, don't give up! Never give up! Be lovingly patient. Stay calm and don't panic. Above all things pray without ceasing.

Teachers need to know that children 10 to 14 react as though their parents are not "with it." But they still need their parents very much, and in their own way, they love them, although at times they are not willing to admit it. Many of them act as though they don't want any hint of parental affection. Yet they need to know that the parent is supportive in spite of parent actions or children's actions. They get security from unconditional parental love. Yet many in their culture act as though they want no parents and teachers in their lives at all. The more the teachers and parents understand each other's problems, the more effective they can be.

A very difficult problem to control is that of extreme dress styles. The early adolescent is just beginning to assert independence. This is done by preferring things the Christian adult world doesn't like. Modesty and neatness may not be in their vocabulary. The Christian school can have dress codes so that they will conform at school, but how do you get them to prefer decent clothes and to make wise choices at other times? It is the rare early adolescent who doesn't skirt the edge in clothing styles, hair styles, street language, their interests, or of their choice of peer group. They constantly test limits.

Parents need to be especially alert to the friends chosen at this time, to try to guide the early adolescent away from the undesirable ones. Parents should not assume that families of their children's friends are upright. Find out what they stand for. Get acquainted with them. Encourage friends who have values similar to your own. Know your community "hang-outs." Know who goes there. Keep in touch with other parents. If you don't, your children will use you as an excuse to do things you won't approve, meaning kids will lie, "My parents said it was okay. They are cool." Then there are kids who whine, "Let me do what I want to do. My parents are so cruel and unreasonable." Be alert to excuses.

When I was a principal of a private school, in the Philippines, one time upon enrolling two boys, their well-dressed parents said, "Thank goodness we are now more than 10,000 miles away from our last school. We can start our boys' social life over again. Our children made such bad choices for friends." I told those parents that we would do our best to help these boys choose better friends. I then proceeded to appoint dynamic student leaders to introduce them and get them involved in the school. By noontime, they had found troublesome friends, even in a select private school—with much the same interests and habits as the group they had left behind. This type of student is everywhere, at select private schools, public schools, and even Christian schools.

This family had missed the boat. Their children were already in high school, and didn't have a middle school experience to allow them to grow up before having to make important decisions for themselves. They needed a significant adult to guide them at a younger age, in order to learn how to make wise peer choices. Sometimes this significant adult is the youth leader, sometimes a teacher, and sometimes a family friend.

In some situations parents have been able with good results to tell early adolescents to use their restrictions as a reason for not doing something their children know is not right according to the family rules. For the most part, this ploy won't work for this exploring age level, unless the parents have developed an unusually strong relationship with their children.

I have tried to emphasize in this chapter that what happens to middle level children at this age level has lifetime consequences. Well-meaning parents can surely foul things up by not establishing a good relationship with them before they get to this age. The trauma they are going through in puberty is taxing on their parents, teachers, themselves, and others responsible for them. The patterns of behavior exhibited by early adolescents at this age, are not easy for them to control. But they are controllable. A note of encouragement. In this impressionable age, they may have scorned and seemingly deserted the right, but there can be a future return. They need to know that the adults important to them never desert them. They need adults who are loyal and have faith in them, while emphasizing responsibility, honesty, loyalty, grooming, morality, and religious principles, in a non-threatening, Christlike way.

They don't understand themselves because so many changes are happening to their bodies and to their lives at the same time. In my speeches I have used the example of a pregnant woman, who at times, loses control of her emotions and reactions, crying when there is no obvious reason to cry. So many things were happening to her body that she was not herself. So it is with 10 to 14-year-old students. A friend upon reading this said, "This makes me laugh because crying without reason is a regular part of being myself. Many women have the same experience, when they've been pregnant." Which in essence means, don't come to hasty conclusions. Weigh all of the facts. We need to be sympathetic to these changes and help these children develop well.

At good middle schools, this is understood and they educate their faculties accordingly. In its 1995 handbook, a public middle school lists characteristics that the faculty developed from their years of experience with early adolescents. A few are:

Intellectual Development (edited):
Students in the middle years—
Are in transition from concrete to abstract
Prefer active over passive experiences
Are often preoccupied with self
Have a strong need for approval
May be easily discouraged
Are inquisitive about adults, often challenging their
    authority. Always observing them.

Physical Development:
    Students in their middle years—
    Experience rapid, irregular physical growth
    Undergo bodily changes that may cause awkward, unco-
        ordinated behavior
    Have varying maturity rates with girls tending to mature
        one and one-half to two years earlier than boys . . .
    Experience restlessness and fatigue due to hormonal
        changes
    Need daily physical activity because of increased energy
    Experience significant brain growth, followed by a period
        of non-growth, with girls generally undergoing
        change earlier than boys.
    Are concerned with sexual maturation and changes result-
        ing in an increase in nose size, protruding ears, long
        arms, and awkward posture.

    Remember the children 10 to 14 don't care for complica-
tions of these changes any more than you do. True professionals have the desire to set an environment that makes the
adjustment less traumatic. It will always be difficult for this
growing age group. However, if helped properly, they will be
able to handle the next level (adolescence) better if they learn
well how to survive this age. With the knowledge expressed in
this chapter, teachers, youth leaders, parents, and other adults,
ought to realize in what type of environment these youngsters
flourish. Thus they can develop middle schools true to the
concept, for 10 to 14-year-old children, who then will grow into
healthy teenagers. That is the main goal of every middle school,
secular and Christian. If we meet this goal then we'll no longer
be able to say, "Stuck in the Middle."

Questions

1. What are the characteristics of a school unique for 10 to 14-year-old children?
2. What do you consider five of the most important behaviors common to this age level? How would you as a teacher attempt to resolve them?
3. What ten characteristics do you think teachers should find most important in understanding this age level?
4. What is the danger of being legalistic and over-reacting to these characteristics peculiar to early adolescents?

2
Character Development—Values

Middle level students are influenced by others with whom they interact. Is it too late for the middle school to help early adolescents begin to assume responsibility for focusing on character development, which includes making wise choices? Is it a good time for early adolescents to begin making some choices for themselves? Should the middle school ignore this, and stick to the basics? Does the set of values that they learn help them in the choices they make?

We believe that morals should be incorporated with subject matter. How could a Christian school not conceive of such an idea? A good teacher realizes that students need the help of values in developing character. We exist in order to produce students who practice Christian values. What good is an educated person void of character? At this age level it is possible to influence patterns of behavior. The student's set of values coalesce to form the nucleus of his character. In a Christian school, it is exciting to see believers' values taught. These are scripturally defined, and there is unanimity in them. Parents should give full support to them.

What are these values that, if learned well, enable the students to exhibit character decision-making and leadership? Some of them follow:

Honesty
Self respect

Loyalty
Courtesy
Fairness
Courage
Responsibility
Cooperation
Initiative
Promptness
Gentleness
Morality
Persistence
Prayerful
Trustworthy
Cleanliness
Respect
Discernment

Imagine the impact of exposing children to teaching that includes a consciousness of these character-building traits. It makes teaching that much more rewarding. Some would say these should be taught in the home and schools should stick to academic subjects. True, the home should teach these. The Christian school is working in harmony with the home, reinforcing and extending these values. What a beautiful concept! They work together. Every effort should be made in every classroom and everywhere else under the control of the school to enhance the development of character. In this character development area, we need to know where each individual seems to be in this process. It may be difficult, as there are no acceptable concrete measurements that we can use. Yet it is incumbent on the Christian teacher to be aware of where a youngster has character flaws, and work to improve them.

Here is where true individual differences are visible. Even though we recognize that the teaching of a value may not be one hundred percent successful, we do know the results are better when character development is not ignored. We also believe that there are delayed results, which will show later in a student's life. The world needs people of character who are true to biblical practices in their daily lives at home, at school, at work, and at play. The school and home are partners in promoting those things that build character. They are mutually respectful of each other. Their roles are clearly scripturally designed. Evangelicals, believing that the Bible is the inerrant Inspired Word of God, arrive at these conclusions naturally.

Students are not in a vacuum. Others, outside the home and school, also influence these children. Neighbors, friends, church youth leaders, and the community as a whole contribute either positively or negatively to the formation of a student's character. These influences must be considered too. Our Lord was the perfect model. He was always taking care of others' needs. Christians with character use their talents to benefit others. This is contrary to the current ME generation attitude to which the students are constantly exposed. If believers succeed in developing good values, then with strengthened social skills, they can present the gospel of Jesus Christ effectively. Christian schools should refine their goals and methods to be more effective in teaching character. What people affect character?

Peers: A strong influence.
Teachers: An invaluable influence.
Family: No doubt, the most important influence.
Minorities: Need to improve thoughts about them.
Persecuted: Need to stand up to injustice.
Others with whom they come in contact:
This can't be controllable.

The list of influences is endless. Perhaps you can think of more. Teachers and others responsible for this age level need to remember the impact of these influences when planning classroom lessons. Consciousness of what to look for helps teachers focus on what is or is not being achieved.

In order to have a program that will build character, the middle school teacher needs a carefully drawn-up design in each content course in order to know how to help these students realize the importance of character, not just in general development, or in spiritual growth, but in one's individual personal development, as well. Early adolescents can show their lack of character by being very crude, by not standing up for what is right, by being unfair to the handicapped, by forming a clique rejecting a good friend, by purposely showing disrespect, by using foul language, by showing off for the crowd, and in many other ways. Unguided, they will love a person and at the same time do nasty things, probably while others watch. This is a distinct character flaw.

We repeat that they can suddenly ignore a friend. They can be impossible and unreasonable without cause. They can be unreasonably silly. They can be disloyal to a long-time friend. Teachers need to be aware that teachers themselves can precipitate this type of behavior by establishing certain negative situations, even though students are born again.

What I'm saying is: poor teachers exist everywhere. Teachers lack character too. They tend to blame the students for a poorly run class. Because all students were born in sin and shaped in iniquity, it is all the more necessary for teachers to set up positive character-building situations. Students must grow in character so that they won't be characterless when fighting against the odds. They will grow to see beyond the worldly view of their society. Students who develop the personal values (character traits) recommended in this chapter, with the accompanying social skills, will show real Christlike character when needed. They will stand out in their community.

Unfortunately, most students in middle school are not that

far along. They desperately need good modeling and good instruction in every aspect. This is real guidance at work. The expression of Christian values, which become a part of their daily actions, results in character at its best. This is lacking in secular education. They need to handle opposing views with grace.

There still is need for a guidance specialist to help them with individual problems and to help teachers in the guidance process. Who can teach character better than those who have the students most of the day? Many children spend longer weekly hours with teachers than with parents. What needs do Christian students have? Many of these needs are similar to their secular counterparts.

Some students, even from so-called Christian homes, come from situations in which they learned few or no standards. They have to be taught. Parents learn from students too and are blessed by what they are being taught. A school that is guidance-minded through and through makes a positive difference in the students. Parents who are having difficulty understanding the early teens appreciate any help they can get from a guidance-oriented school.

Character is elusive to parents and educators. Many times they don't know what it is. Its components need clarification. Commonly agreed-on goals need to be set. We need to know what common goals we are trying to achieve. The home and school can learn much from each other in the attempt to identify these goals more accurately. Parents and teachers need mutual reinforcement. This is one area in which Christian schools can excel. The end product, the students, should show by their lives the result of character teaching. The test is: do they show it?

No, early adolescence is not too late in life to begin a consciousness of good character. A great deal of in-service training is needed for the teachers to model and teach good character. Imagine the impact an effective character program could have on society.

Questions

1. What are the components of character?
2. Why are they so rarely systematically taught in secular schools? Why don't Christian schools do more?
3. Can you describe the student who exhibits character?
4. Why is it important that it be incorporated in all subjects, in the school, including lunchroom, hallways, and play areas?
5. What goals could you set in the subject you teach that would improve character in your students?

3

The Most Important Cog in the Wheel: The Teacher

The middle school is justified on the premise that this developmental level demands a teacher who understands that there are special characteristics a middle school student has that require of the teacher special knowledge and attention. The professional responsible for the middle level student needs to be someone who can roll with the punches and come back with an acceptable response. For example, in one middle school classroom a student said, "You don't look as bad today as you did yesterday." To which the teacher replied, "Thank you, Jeremy. I feel good, too."

That ended it. The teacher was self-confident enough to respond to the student without a long lecture. She certainly was not majoring in the minors. If the student persists and continually harasses the teacher, then private disciplinary action is necessary. But they need someone who does not get affronted by a crude response that is clumsy and awkward. Teachers shouldn't excuse the response or ignore it. Handle it tactfully and appropriately to this age level. Stay cool and remember you are the adult in this situation. Show calm maturity. Teachers who have "hang-ups" in their own lives will use unsatisfactory responses, such as sarcasm, put-downs, screaming and excessive lecturing, sending to office, and "write this sentence one hundred times."

Such actions turn students away from the teacher, and the teacher's value as a significant adult decreases dramatically. One rule of the thumb is: avoid embarrassing students even when disciplining. Deal with each student individually by casually and calmly walking up and quietly clearing up the situation. Students need you to help them decide what is acceptable behavior.

Sometimes students misbehave in class because the teachers set an atmosphere that is not conducive to good behavior. The students respond negatively to the teacher who plans poorly, allows too much idle time, and seems indifferent to students. The students respond to a confused class atmosphere, and then get punished for it. Middle level students are quick to react and quick to appreciate teachers who know how to set a proper classroom climate. They will respond accordingly, you can be sure. The attitude of teachers, hired for middle schools, toward early adolescents (and their innovative creativeness) must take precedence over credit accumulation, content mastery, years of experience or college attended.

Administrators should look for subtle signs during the interview that convince administrators that these teachers would do well with 10 to 14-year-old students. Will this teacher major in the minors, when students misbehave, and fly off in a tantrum because the students slump in their chairs or do some other minor thing natural to this growing age? The smart teachers "pick their fights." This is an not appeal to overlook disciplinary problems. It is an appeal for teachers to avoid creating them. Administrators will find it less difficult if they do well at bringing together a faculty that is committed to this age level.

Besides balanced classroom management, a middle school staff must have teachers who have advanced knowledge in their subjects, knowledge of the basic skills, and, most of all, knowledge in growth and development. What a staff that would be! No single teacher can have all of these, but a balanced faculty can. In this way middle schools can handle an ever-widening homogeneous group. The better our instruction, the less narrowly homogeneous the students will become. I don't mean the staff should be all of one type. How dull that would be. Students learn by adjusting to all types. I am asking that teachers respect each other and avoid criticizing one another.

A balanced teaching staff would have the subject matter knowledge that the school needs. The teachers possess knowledge of their subject with a balance of a good mental hygiene toward students. Some schools are located in areas where the student body is very capable. Such a school will have all of these basic needs on the staff, plus additional subject matter specialists. The students need knowledgeable teachers as they are approaching difficult content, since the students already possess a smattering of knowledge, which demands teachers who can help them synthesize it.

I would next consider in the interview process the methods the teacher uses in the classroom. Are they monotonous, dull routine? Do they have variety? How successful would the methods be for the early adolescent? Are interesting, exciting multimedia resources used? Are multi-media presentations appropriate or relied upon as something to do? What types of projects for this age level are planned? How is homework handled? How much weight do teachers give to any one area when grading? These and many other questions will tell administrators much as to how the subjects will be taught, and how appropriate prospective teachers would be for middle level students. Future chapters will deal with the effective use of multi-media, projects, and homework.

It is true that some subjects lend themselves more to variety than others. All classrooms need different media and methods to interact. Creative teachers supply some variety no matter what the subject.

Social Studies (history), for example, can use a combination of methods very effectively. A precaution here is necessary. Don't vary teaching practices because they're expected. There must be good reasons for every method used. Use the most effective one for that moment and topic. Getting back to social studies, a combination of total class discussion, small group discussion, debates, research, projects, memorization, oral and written reports, games, all kinds of art projects, and even occasional lectures can be very wholesome and effective. Also available in this technologically advanced age are guest speakers, films, and all sorts of visual aids. Cooperative teaching strategies lend themselves well to this area.

Well-trained and successful teachers have a wealth of methods available. Keep in mind that the main purpose of these methods is to impart accurate knowledge while teaching students to use those skills demanded by modern civilization. Studies have indicated that the more a student is involved in the learning process, the more knowledge and skill he will learn. Keep them involved.

Science is another subject that allows for a wide range of methods. Many of these will be hands-on experiments. With the scientific process, students can learn the value of the scientific method in everyday life. They will also be able to see its limitations. Writing up scientific observations accurately is another important skill, as are measuring accurately. observing accurately, and recording accurately. These are valuable skills that far transcend the science classroom.

When observing, the administrator should know the content skills and timing goals of the class. Administrators must help teachers keep on task. Successful teachers I have known had thirteen elements in common. They would be appropriate for any middle school. Use them wisely. I observed most of these elements in all successful classrooms.

1. As Pestalozzi says, keep "a firm but kind discipline." Example: Sarcastically or icily, the teacher asks, "Where is your homework? You are grounded for recess today. Do you hear me?" Next it's made general, tackling everybody. "Class, I don't know how you expect to be successful if you don't do your homework. Nobody can pass my course without doing homework! Get it!"

That was an example of a poor discipline technique, baiting. Here is an understanding, firm, but polite discipline:

I can't believe your homework is not done. I'm sorry to see you have to stay in for lunch today, but that is what happens when the homework is not done. It's just too bad.

Empathy, firmness, non-embarrassing comments avoid triggering the rebellious attitude so common to early adolescents. I observed both these situations.

2. Show respect for your students, and they will show respect for you. For example: Ask students or class for forgiveness when you "blow it." Remember the tone of your voice says much.
3. Be consistent. If you make a decision, stick with it, unless you made a mistake.

We all make mistakes at times. One teacher admitted such a mistake to me. She said, "I made the mistake of allowing the math class, when spring was approaching, to go outside the first warm day. I didn't clarify the rules by saying we would not be going out again. Every day until June, I was asked if we were going outside. I was kind but not firm or consistent."

4. Exhibit enthusiasm for the task.
5. Be flexible and open to change. Caution: Do not let them manipulate you.
6. Know your content and what you want to do for each lesson. Be prepared. Don't teach, "off the cuff."
7. Have a sense of humor. Help them understand your humor. Be sure it is in good taste. Don't let it dominate the situation. Perhaps this is one of the most important tools of teachers.
8. Enjoy their company. Participate in interest areas with them. Teaching is fun!
9. Don't talk down to them, even when they act like little children.
10. Don't let them get your goat, or make you cry. You are the adult; act like it. They get security from that.
11. Establish a relationship with parents. You are not in this alone.
12. Be honest with your principal, parents, and students. Remember to keep the principal well informed of even the slightest problem.
13. Be fair. Treat all students fairly. Some will be easier than others to be fair to.

These valuable suggestions, if taken seriously, will make teaching in middle school a pleasure. They come from my experience as a teacher, principal, college professor, and administrator of middle schools, and from my co-author's middle school teaching experiences. In various positions I had to form a staff, supervise teachers, plan and conduct in-service programs, help middle school principals, and formulate curriculum. Such wealth of experience should produce something of value for the reader.

Christian teachers in a middle school should be willing to subscribe to the following beliefs. They are essential for the school to be an effective middle school. These beliefs are good reminders of what we, in middle school education, are all about. They focus our attention. Christian students go through the same developmental stages as worldly ones. The physical, emotional, and mental changes happen to everyone, but in different ways. The effects are the same. But these changes can be less traumatic in a good Christian middle school. The staff has to arrive at common beliefs. They can do this on in-service days.

The staff believes that:

There is a need for a specific school to take care of the child 10 to 14.

The preadolescent is in a rapidly growing developmental period.

All children do not grow in unison at the same rate. A teacher can't assume maturity in other areas, just because some grew physically. It is possible to have a physically mature, emotional pygmy, and vice versa. This growth variety requires teachers who feel good about themselves and have a rich academic background.

A settled, firm, lively, flexible, caring, environment, controlled by professionals, is needed.

Middle school teachers need to be competent, academically superior professionals, thoroughly knowledgeable of this developmental age level.

Middle school students should be free from excessive pressure and inappropriate competition. In this area the following ought to be given serious thought: No highly competitive interscholastic teams. If handled properly teams can be an asset. They can improve skills, build confidence, and teach loyalty among other things. Avoid overly emotional stress.

No final exams covering weeks of work. Grades should not depend on one big test or project.

Frequent grading periods such as every six weeks, work best with this age.

No sophisticated adult-type social activities. The more informal the better. Youth leaders need to remember this, too!

The staff further believes that:

Peer groups are of primary importance, affecting attitudes, interests, choice of friends, and clothing styles.

This is the time for a solid general education for all students. In addition, exceptional students should receive other content they need, advanced as well as remedial courses.

The 10 to 14-year-old is at an opportune age to develop values. The staff should identify which values to emphasize. (Parents should welcome the effort: honesty, tolerance, acceptance of ideas, respect, persistence, graciousness, courteousness, humility, confidence, consistency, personal cleanliness, manliness and womanliness, morality, ethics, and thankfulness). These are but a few that make a person stand out. This is a time to expand student horizons beyond just the basics. The mini-course program takes care of this. This used to be known as the extra-curricular program.

Middle school teachers can make a difference. But we have not totally arrived. Teaching in a middle school is exciting, as it continually changes to be more suitable to this age group. What a challenge! There is always need for improvement.

Middle schools ought to be significantly different from

elementary and secondary school, because the students are different. Teachers need to recognize and believe that. In this formative, transitional stage of life, adult culturing and careful guidance are needed, but not dominance.

Middle school administrators must exert a consistent, firm, kind discipline. Administrators should show an authority that can be respected. They are important role models. How they handle crises and other situations will influence students and staff for either good or bad. Under good administrative leadership, we believe the middle school students will perform as they truly should be better prepared for high school than as if they took a set of required subjects in a secondary style environment. They will be better adjusted to handle the academic and social rigors of high school.

In summary, permit us to call some matters of importance to the attention of middle school teachers. This is done for emphasis. Please excuse the repetition. Teachers, keep these transitional children ever before you. You are teachers for their benefit. Understand that they are undergoing rapid and erratic change. They are not in control of their changes. They unknowingly need your help, and are clumsy at acknowledging it. These changes cause them to be tired and apparently lazy one day, overactive and playful the next day, and reliably normal the rest of the time. The exasperating thing is that they don't go through this at the same time. Remember, if they're not handled properly, behavior problems will arise, limiting the opportunity for them to learn.

The last thing middle school teachers want to do is to further complicate the students' lives. Do not overly tease them or continually frustrate them. Believe it or not, they are a rewarding delight to teach. They are positively responsive to their teachers. What happens to them will have either a positive or negative influence for a long time. Teachers need to keep in mind that their students are not at this developmental stage by choice. They would just as soon skip it. However, they must go through this process to develop properly. Our job, as professionals, is not to prevent them from going through it, but to help them through it, and not to complicate their lives more in school.

I've felt the students would be better off having the three years off school, rather than have to go through the horrible experiences of a poorly conducted middle school. Yes! The teacher is the most important cog in the wheel. Without the dedication of the total staff to the beliefs expressed in this chapter, the school would be an empty shell. If you stay with it long enough, you will be able to see the results of your endeavors.

Questions

1. Why is it so important that middle school teachers be thoroughly knowledgeable of human growth and development?
2. Is it true that after a middle school child is saved (born again) that he has no more growth problems? Explain.
3. What teacher characteristics need to be exhibited in order for teachers to be good middle level role models?
4. What should the teacher keep in mind when considering the appropriate methods for this age level? Be specific.
5. What should be significantly different about being a Christian middle school teacher?
6. How is teaching like being a missionary?

4

Why a Christian Middle School?

Basis for Curriculum Development

A curriculum is more than a list of subjects. A school curriculum is everything that happens to the student under the guidance of the school. Learning takes place as a part of their experiences, in the halls, at lunch, on the playground, as well as in the classroom. Effective schools try to ensure that these favorable experiences are beneficial lessons. A Christian school must not underestimate the importance of a good school environment. The total school is the curriculum, and it can teach students the essence of Christianity.

In the formal subjects, a middle school is not merely preparation for senior high. The middle school curriculum and practices shouldn't be dictated by high school expectations. A good middle school will automatically meet those expectations and more. If the students have a pleasant middle school working experience, they will enjoy tackling high school subjects. Pressures do exist from parents and even some misguided educators to sometimes offer high school courses "en masse" in the middle school. This is not appropriate to the struggling early adolescent. Sometimes these courses are an "ego trip" for parents who demand them, whether their children are ready or not!

It is a known fact that very few middle school students would benefit from taking a high school course, such as geometry. Most have enough problems growing up. Their bodies, including the mind, are undergoing radical changes, causing them not to understand themselves at times. Many a teacher remembers middle school students who took advanced courses and made A's, but when they got to high school, they seemingly couldn't remember the material. There are those who say that the brain doesn't grow at a steady rate any more than the rest of the physical body does, and that there is a resting time at the middle school level. Whatever the reason, students could learn the material much more readily and with a lot less hassle if we would just be patient and wait for the developmental process to take place. God made that process too!

Why rush students? Do we want to make life less enjoyable? There is a maturity that has nothing to do with whether or not students can "regurgitate" content. That is not real learning, anyway. Can the student apply the learned material? Does the learner see and apply relationships? Even in a Christian middle school with a select enrollment, these types of advanced offerings must be the exception, not the rule. Otherwise, the advanced subjects offered will have to be watered down to a nothingness. Plan challenging work proper to their age level. There is so much untouched knowledge they could pursue.

Now, let us consider some subject-specific areas.

Science—and the Christian School

In the secular school, science is king. Current society places great emphasis upon it. Its importance to modern-day society cannot be minimized. The Christian middle school student needs to be well-versed in the scientific progress being made in our society. In addition, the students must be knowledgeable in scientific methods, becoming scientists in their own right. As Christians we must not be afraid of the claims of science, but instead we must know how to discard unproven claims. Ignorance of science will affect the future of the students in testing and in the world of work. Misinterpretations of our values and beliefs often prevent Christian school students from becoming good scientists. To become outstanding scientists, our students must know Christianity and science.

Often the Christian school is in danger of teaching more about the Science we are against than about authentic secular science. As long as we live in such a diverse society, our students need to be well versed in worldly scientific knowledge. They must know the secular view of science before they can intelligently refute it. They also need good science instruction to qualify for college by passing standardized tests made by secular educators. Christian parents need to be assured that knowing that data is not equivalent to believing it.

Christian students can learn much by applying the scientific method. They need to know its shortcomings and its assets. We must teach students worldly methods and knowledge about science and also how to use experiments to God's glory. Let us admit as Christians that every day in our lives we are blessed with products produced and improved by science. It's not all bad! Let us keep in mind our goal, which is to develop scientists who will become the best scientists possible, yet not violate God's laws, morally or otherwise. Another primary and useful goal is to demolish the commonly accepted secular myths, and then work with the rest. As Christians, we need to educate a generation that will exert a positive influence on the scientific community.

Therefore, we need to advocate a program that thoroughly covers the whole spectrum of science in the three years of middle school. Christian schools have nothing to fear in the teaching of science. Our students must not become anti-science. But they must learn to distinguish truth from fiction. They must oppose the wrong false assumptions upon which wrong conclusions are made. Society will eventually be thankful for individuals who can do this. As Christians, the students must learn how to use scientific tools to make new discoveries and to improve life on earth. We can see our learning in the perspective of the Christian world view. As a result, our students should learn more than the secular student, for they need to know both viewpoints, secular and Christian.

Foreign Languages and the Christian School

Of all the people on the earth, Christians ought to be the most favorable to a multicultural and multilingual curriculum. Our mandate from our Lord makes it important. The Christian school should have a strong program. Serious investigations into new ways to teach language and other cultures are needed. We need to steep our students in the knowledge of foreign languages and cultures. Having a language class is no longer enough. We should use modern technology and its benefits, to bring us into contact with other languages and cultures. Our emphasis should be on communication. Our students will need to know the culture and its subtleties, so they can communicate with people.

The world is getting smaller. Learning to understand foreign languages and cultures helps Christian students no matter what occupation they choose. What better witness could there be than one who is able to appreciate the language of a people and empathize with their culture? Whether we like it or not, the world is getting smaller, and it is imperative that we understand it.

What does all of this background have to do with a middle school language program? I believe the middle school's role is to develop an appreciation of the language groups of the world. American students need to recognize the values of other cultures. They also need to understand how language is developed. They need to have respect for other languages and cultures. They could learn one language in depth, but that's not important until high school. A few advanced ones can do that in middle school. The important thing is to develop a favorable attitude toward people who use other languages at home and abroad.

Offering exploratory courses would be a step in the right direction. These would be in much more depth than is typical today. They should cover areas common to the learning of most languages and cultures. They can study in depth later in high school. It is recommended that students struggling with the basics of the English language be denied permission to study some other language. The rudiments of English are difficult enough for anybody.

Students should have enough language exposure to know whether or not foreign language study is to their liking. I can't say it often enough: high interest makes for good learning, especially for the student in middle school.

Bible—God's Word

There is no subject more important than the Bible. Therefore the Bible books to be studied and the topics to be learned need to be carefully chosen. Bible courses require the use of as much creativity as other courses. The tendency to lapse into sermonizing must be avoided. A Bible course is successful, if, as a result of taking the course, the students refer to the Bible for answers to life's problems and voluntarily read it daily. The aim is to teach content in an interesting fashion, and to make applications to daily life. The teacher's desire is to teach the relevance of the Scriptures. True, not all is relevant at any one time to one person. Some of it must be stored for later application. Methods include small group interaction, projects, presentations, individual investigation, memorizing verses, Bible drills, question and answers, and use of resources.

As the result of taking a Bible class, students should know how to find their way around the Bible, how to use references, and how to use other resources. Most of all they should recognize its importance to life.

The school needs to establish goals for the teaching of the Bible. These should be such things as that:

1. Students will use the Bible daily.
2. Students will know how to find their way around the Bible.
3. Students will use references and other resources.
4. Students will be knowledgeable of major events.
5. Students will understand the major doctrines presented.
6. Students will be encouraged to ask questions (how, where, when, who, why) leading to personal application.

These and many more will make Bible classes more unified in purpose, and guarantee thorough coverage.

Social Studies—History

Whether a middle school uses the Social Studies approach or the more traditional historical approach depends on the traditions of the school. At all costs the methods of the teachers need to contain the many approaches that make this subject so effective. They will need a variety of methods. These subjects lend themselves to group activities very well. There is a tendency for some teachers daily to lapse into straight lecture. Exclusive use of this method is inappropriate for the early adolescent. A combination of group activities, sprinkled with lecture, class discussion, projects, field trips, resource people, reading of primary documents, and community service work will aid the student's curiosity and learning.

The basic principles of American democracy should be explored and thoroughly understood. It is a good age to learn American history. This age level is affected by heroes, and this is a good time to present positive role models. It is an age known for fair play, and to build on that early adolescent characteristic makes the curriculum much more valuable. Social Studies—History presents an opportunity for the Christian school to discuss ethics, morality, bravery, sacrifice, and endless other values.

It's a time for learning the valuable skills of research, effective communicating, organizing material, sifting facts, drawing conclusions, taking notes, and verifying data. In addition, just think of all the communication skills a student can learn. Additional skills include listening accurately, voice control, persuasiveness, confidence, use of emotion, and a multitude of other valuable skills.

If there ever was a time when Christians needed to know how to forcibly present an argument and to organize ideas intelligently, it is today. Christian school students need to learn these things if they are going to be a positive influence in society. Otherwise we are rearing them for a monastic lifestyle where they will be isolated and clustered to themselves.

Knowledge of the world around them is important, too. In the middle school, this curriculum should include a time to learn local, state, and U.S. history. Knowing these functions will help them be more active participants in society than previous generations.

The curriculum then can be expanded to their neighboring countries and the world. An understanding of geography would be helpful. They ought to understand maps and how to read different ones. The possibilities are endless. In all aspects they need to learn the Christian role in life, what it should be, and what they can do. They shouldn't merely study about history, but also live parts of it. Their classes should be more than recitation from textbooks. That's good in itself, but it is not adequate in the development of an activist Christian scholar. These subjects don't merely teach what happened, but also, in the light of what's happened, how to be an effective citizen. What could be more important for students to learn?

English/Language Arts—Reading/Writing/Speaking

A middle school needs to look at this subject through the sequence of language development, oral language development to listening development, reading development, and writing development. Using this approach prevents the program from putting the cart before the horse. Middle school students need to cement the basics while they have access to knowledgeable teachers. Middle schools should make sure the children know their skills. To ascertain where they are in the basics, tests may be used that determine what basic skill they have not achieved. Example: "The student knows how to spell daily-used words. The student has no difficulty reading basic materials." Therefore, reading instruction is advanced for that student. Teachers familiar with the skills needed by middle school students can identify the need.

It is necessary for the Christian to be an effective communicator orally and in writing. This portion of the three R's must not be overlooked. To be a communicator takes a combination of rote memory and practice. Too much emphasis on either one will cause failure. A competent person in the English language can spell, use grammatically correct language, read well, and generally know how to correct mistakes. Long, written projects are verboten. They encourage bad habits. Short, to-the-point papers are much better for this age. The papers must be long enough to show glaring mistakes. Frequent exposure to writing exercises helps. Students respond well if their written assignments deal with topics of high interest to them. It is not an age requiring long and cumbersome projects.

This is the age of reading for pleasure, believe it or not. They love to read books on their level, though not what you think they should read. Classics can be on their level. Each individual has different interests. Making a variety of books available is commendable. If possible, set some class time aside periodically for reading and sharing what is read. There ought to be a mixture of classics and current books. In these days it is advisable, when studying literature, to have a group of parents read the books first to guarantee that offensive language and ideas are not used. If such is used, the teacher may present it in such a way that the offensive language will be understood in its context.

Students at this age also love to be read to. Read to them. Try a long story that they are not likely to read for themselves. It should be something of high interest, have some challenging vocabulary, and a plot that's complicated enough to need interpreting. This should be a fun learning activity and students should not be tested on it. Much learning can ensue from this as the class discusses the plot and the related ideas.

English/Language Arts are important to parents. They love to see their middle schoolers read, write effectively, and communicate well. Reading instruction is a part of the Language Arts program in the middle school. Students usually have a separate period for reading instruction. They can learn basic reading, vocabulary development, and speed reading. Middle school students must be able to read well enough to do their own homework. Good reading instruction will be a tremendous value to the students. The middle school is accountable for seeing that the students master the basics, not only in reading but in all subjects. Otherwise they belong in remedial programs, which should take precedence over advanced mathematics, such as Algebra I and/or foreign language. A good English/Language Arts program is another important program in the middle school. The basics can and should be cemented in middle school by teachers who know how to correct flaws and teach new elements.

Will students know how to speak effectively, read well, and write decently, as a result of the English/Language Arts curriculum? Set up the goals for what we want to achieve and then set out to accomplish them. Don't let the textbooks dictate this!

Mathematics

There is a great controversy over whether or not middle school students benefit from taking advanced mathematics. Many times they can perform the functions, but there are three big questions. Is their mental process developed enough to fully perform the functions required for abstract mathematics? Can they remember essential data when performing advanced math in high school? Also, can they remember the functions needed to pass the SATs or the equivalent? The answer is yes and no. Yes for the rare student who should have taken advanced math in middle school, and NO to the many who shouldn't have but who took it, to satisfy parents or to fill sections. Again we ask, "What's the rush?"

The recent experience of a middle school mathematics

teacher who taught the top .03 percent of the students in a suburban school, presents a caution to the reader. These students took Algebra I in the sixth grade, Geometry in the seventh grade, and Algebra II in the eighth grade. They definitely had the ability to pass the course, but at what cost? Is it worth it? Several had to quit horseback riding lessons, Little League, band, or chorus to be able to keep up. Then in high school, they were propelled into even higher math classes, so they quit mathematics. They had their required Carnegie Units for mathematics. Why? Why? Society rates a school on how many students are in these courses, but schools should be rated on what is best for the early adolescent.

Should a middle school student take Algebra I and/or Geometry? Most middle schoolers should not! Those who are ready for it, Yes. For the student who is naturally a mathematics person, fine. Notice I didn't say the student who excelled in another subject. Math and other subjects differ as to what they require of the student. This whole venture should be approached with caution. Constant supervision is necessary.

The rest of the mathematics curriculum can be filled with challenges, from general mathematics to accounting, to statistics, and even algebraic expressions. This rich offering will enable the students to hone their skills and learn new ones without developing negative attitudes toward mathematics and learning. They won't have to give up those activities that serve them well in their growing childhood.

In some forms of skill development and general math a limited amount of ability grouping is warranted. No groups should have students so limited that there is no built-in motivation, within the group. They need some successful students to carry the group. Teachers feel that way too. Students learn much when the class is structured so that they can learn from each other. The teacher has to gauge that.

Again, middle school is a good time to check out the

basics. Teachers are trained to correct problems. Students need to work on these while they still have teachers expert in diagnosing and prescribing for them.

The Related Arts—High Tech—Rounding Out Education

There is another area of knowledge stressed in middle school, the Related Arts area. These are co-ed. Boys and girls both need to know the basics of cooking and girls need to know the basics of repairs required of everyone in the twenty-first century. They need to know budgeting, cooking, cleaning, repairing, physical fitness, dieting, music appreciation, art forms, and crafts. The Related Arts courses include familiar and unfamiliar courses to adults, such as, Home Arts, Wood and Metal working, Physical Education, Art, Music, Sex Education, and Modern Technology. Knowledge and appreciation of these subjects expands the developing early adolescents' experiences. A life void of these areas is an empty life. They are essential parts of living in today's world, as so many young people are leaving their families and establishing a household before marrying. This is true of Christian students too. Sometimes their occupations take them far away from home where they need to know what to do independently.

These subjects should never be decreed as unimportant. The skills learned have tremendous impact and will prove valuable in life. The person who can cook meals and repair belongings will have a distinct advantage over the person who can't.

In these days, having healthy physical bodies and knowing how to take care of them is vitally important. Having physical education contributes to a strong body, which leads to strong mental health. Being able to do things around the house, helps with the family budget. Also, as leisure time becomes more available these subjects become even more valuable. Peoples' time should not be frittered away passively watching television. They need to develop hobbies and active interests that will be healthy for them for life. Also, active growing students need movement during the school day. Otherwise they will expend energy in ways that may not be acceptable.

Being aware of the early adolescent's growth factors and what they mean in the educational process is one of the strengths of the middle school. The day must be balanced between activity and mental pursuits. These subjects help.

Spend time some day following a student's schedule to see how proper it is for the growing early adolescent. Is it dull or exciting? Is the day dying of routine, or is it exuberant with excitement? The related arts should be full of activity and excitement.

Another related arts subject in a Christian middle school is family life or sex education. The ever-changing hormone system of the early adolescent requires open and clear explanations. The common curiosity of the changing early adolescent should be handled delicately and frankly. A special Christian program needs to be developed. There are worthy Christian goals in this subject.

Chapelgate Christian Academy in Maryland has such a program, especially designed by a former public school sex education teacher, Mrs. Daryl Drown, for a Christian school. This Christian teacher recognized the need for students to learn these things from the school instead of from the teenaged culture. If there ever was an age level that needed to understand bodily changes and to develop sound moral values related to them, this is it. By all means, give it a priority. Christianize it. God will bless.

Computers—Technology: What is Life without Them?

An important part of living in the twenty-first century is vastness of knowledge that exists and competent use of computers. In this day, a curriculum would be void unless it included how to operate a computer and familiarity with the many ways it can be used for learning and for pleasure. Before the end of the three years in middle school, the student ought to be familiar with the latest programs developed, the Internet, use of modems, how to use computers daily in the home, and with the many changes happening. All fear of using a computer should be alleviated. Not only will shopping, banking, and all sorts of transactions be done by computer, but many functions now reserved to traditional teaching in a school will be creatively incorporated into interactive educational software. Life will be dysfunctional without a computer. So it is with other technologies. The truly educated person will be skilled in the technological changes in their lives.

Guidance: The Heartbeat of a School

To help students adjust to school, especially in middle school, when they are undergoing such severe mental and physical changes, requires a well-developed guidance program. It should not be separated from the regular classroom, except for private individual needs. The guidance counselor must be knowledgeable of and empathetic to this delicate age. The guidance counselor should be available to teachers. The guidance counselor should organize topics for classroom discussions based on student reactions to classroom and society's demands. The guidance counselor should organize the standardized testing program. Tests will have to be ordered, scheduled, administered, scored, and interpreted to teachers, students, and parents. This important function must not be overlooked. If there is no guidance counselor, then the administrator or a teacher needs to be trained to do it. Special training should be made available.

Early adolescents do not understand what's happening to them. Even the adults who are responsible for them are often puzzled by students responses and clumsy actions. They need understanding—not excuses—and guidance by everyone concerned with them. Guidance counselors and classroom teachers should help them overcome obstacles that can seem overwhelming to early adolescents. These children are immature in handling their own problems, and need empathetic adult help. Yes, the curriculum would be void without this built-in function. Of course the guidance counselor should be a committed believer. What a terrific addition to an already guidance-oriented staff!

Summary—Things to Remember

The course titles of a Christian middle school are very similar to those of a secular school. Then what is the difference? The content, viewpoint, and emphasis are different. Content will be viewed from a Christ-centered point of view, rather than a humanistic point of view. This makes a big difference to the Christian parent. The whole way one looks at life is affected. The Christian world view is that there is no ultimate truth outside of God. It then becomes God-centered instead of man-centered. Consistency with the home, the Bible, and the church is the strength of the Christian school.

The curriculum for the middle school must reject the idea that truth can only be experienced here and now. But teachers must also plan to make practical applications when possible. That is, curriculum must contain elements of the world in which the student lives. The curriculum should not complicate life for an already confused early adolescent. Our job is to supply Christian answers and methods on how to cope with life. The Christian middle school can do this best because it is a warm Christlike atmosphere with clearly delineated expectations.

This is the real total curriculum. The early adolescent receives security in a flexibly structured environment. The content studied, though difficult and challenging, must be interesting and organized. The emphasis should be on how we learn, not just on what we learn. The product of a good middle school is a scholar willing and ready to learn, and one who has learned those skills essential to succeed in the academic world and in life itself. The formal curriculum is merely the vehicle through which this is done.

Remember, everything that happens to students teaches them. The more the curriculum can be made meaningful and actively alive, the more the students will learn. The world is your stage. Use it. The curriculum in a Christian setting is the heart of the Christian school and what makes it worthwhile. We must adopt middle school principles and ideals, if we are going to meet our goals as Christian parents and educators. Without them we fall short of the high mark that is set before us. It should no longer be a question of why a Christian middle school, but when. Soon, I hope.

Questions

1. Why have a Christian middle school?
2. What advantages to the Christian parent are there to a Christian middle school?

3. Name ten of the skills, in any subject, that middle schools teach? Are they measurable?
4. How different are the subjects taught, in Christian middle schools from their secular counterparts? Take one subject and explain.
5. Why is it important for the whole staff to be guidance oriented, in a school composed of early adolescents? How can administrators check that?

5

Broadening Lifetime Interests

The middle school has responded emphatically to the programs in the junior high school that were too sophisticated for
youngsters ten to fourteen years of age. The thinking is that the
junior high had skewed activities, inappropriate for the other
students, because adolescents (ninth graders) were in the
student body. Because of the grade level changes being made
when a school became a middle school, it presented an opportunity to rethink the whole activity program, including interscholastic and extracurricular programs. Following are the
conclusions of educators and parents involved in planning for
the younger age level in middle schools.

The first and most difficult problem was eliminating highly
competitive interscholastic athletic programs. This was not
possible in some localities where interscholastic programs were
the religion of the locals. The reasons for eliminating these
programs were both physical and emotional. Early adolescent
youngsters are going through such tremendous physical
changes that their bone structures are not developed enough
to go through the rigor and extra trauma of intensive interscholastic programs. Pediatricians say that their bones are brittle at
this age.

The second reason is emotional. They are not emotionally
equipped to handle the tremendous emotional pressure of an
interscholastic contest. The pressure is too intense in some
communities. Community honor is at stake. From my obser-

vations I would say that even many adults aren't capable of handling these pressures gracefully. In fact, adults are often the real problem. The timing of the games to a casual afternoon lessens adult pressure.

In middle school we recommend physical and emotional competence and healthy growth without stress. Children will have time to grow up. When they do, they will be able to reap the positive results of an interscholastic program. Sports at this age are good for them, as long as they are free from undue pressure. We didn't say there should be no pressure. As a side benefit interscholastic games will not be "old hat" to them when they get to high school. They then go out for teams with a zest.

Middle schools, without the pressure to win, could teach athletic skills that serve well in high school. It's one thing to play in an informal community club program and another to play in the highly competitive interscholastic program. These community programs can get out of hand, too. Pressures come from parents and other adults. Consequently, well-conducted intramural programs thrive in middle schools. These involve many more children than a single team could. The atmosphere is wholesome. They still have a strong desire to win, but it is within their own world and is more casual. It is the administrator's responsibility to develop a balanced intramural program, free from excessive or abnormal pressure. Such a program is for all students, not just the best athletes. They need coaches capable of teaching the skills needed in life.

Another radical departure from junior high practices is the extracurricular club program. The question is asked, "What is wrong with the club/activity programs of the junior high?" This is not as difficult to change as the interscholastic program. The advocated middle school program of interest areas opens up many more opportunities to middle school youngsters.

Most importantly, the junior high extracurricular program was too limited in its scope. How many new activities will students be introduced to, during school years, in that program? Students were told to sign up for a club, and they remained there all year. In contrast, a middle school program gives the students multiple activities, and more freedom to change interests during the semester. It is much more flexible. Students are free to try an unfamiliar activity without feeling they are sentenced there for a semester or more.

Also there is a wide variety in the types of activities offered. These differ from time to time and faculty to faculty. They are not etched in stone. They depend on the interests of the students and the capability of the faculty and community to lead them. An unexpected advantage is that they create a childlike excitement and break the boredom in a routine school day. A further advantage, is that they enable students to experience and increase competence in a multitude of leisure time activities that will be useful for a lifetime.

Educated people are constantly expanding their interests. Early adolescence is a ripe time to begin expanding lifetime activities. Because it was thought to be beneficial to students at this age, a mini-course program was strongly urged in place of the more rigid extracurricular activity program, of old. This new program's strength is its scope and flexibility. Many good aspects of the club program were retained and supplemented.

Reluctant students were encouraged to try an activity and see how they liked it. They were permitted to drop it if it didn't work out well. Thus, students were encouraged to try a multitude of new activities. They felt free and comfortable trying something to which they were not previously exposed. Therefore, the students were more likely to try new activities. The only regulation was that students had to give it a fair trial. That trial varied with the situation. Students could repeat an activity if they especially enjoyed it. In this way, students could take advantage of numerous activities, while at the same time improving skills in areas they enjoy. Students who do not continue an activity immediately may find it useful later in life. The crucial thing is that they could try the various activities without apprehension or embarrassment.

Given the rapidly changing growth rate of the early adolescent and the growing demands for intensive use of leisure time today, activities developed in the middle school are intended to increase skills, so that as adults they will be encouraged to make wise choices. Developing this mind-set is vital.

The activities offered differ from one school to another, but the objectives will be similar. Offer activities that you have the staff and resources to do. You do not have to duplicate every activity of some other middle school. Instead, concentrate on fulfilling the concept common to middle school.

Just think of the opportunity this informal setting gives for Christian teachers and parents to have an impact on students. If there ever was a time for teachers and parents of conviction to be an influence, it is during these mini-course offerings. The role modeling afforded in these situations is priceless. One can make a difference in the lives of the children who may not realize it, or admit it until much later in life. It is an act of faith. Credit on earth may not be readily available, but our reward will be in Heaven. We do these things not for reward, but because we love. What a privilege.

Contrary to common thinking, early adolescents are not ogres. In an environment that meets early adolescent needs, the students react favorably.

The activities' timing is an important consideration. If the objectives are important to the development of this age group, then starting them on school time and continuing on after school, if necessary, is worthwhile. Caution: This is not a time for turning them "loose." No matter how sophisticated some of them seem, they need supervision (not guards). Having adults in the area would be good. The mere presence of friendly adults prevents problems from developing. The adults can join them and have fun with them. Students appreciate the emotional security of an adult presence. Name-calling, ridicule, poking merciless fun, and even hurting jokes among the adolescents should be controlled.

Sometimes community and church leaders think they need to "rescue" middle schoolers from the restraints of the school, so they sponsor night activities or other activities inappropriate for this age. Youth leaders and others have good intentions. They think they remember the activities they enjoyed at this age. But their memories may have been clouded by time, and the activities may not have been appropriate for them, either. It is important to properly plan activities for a developmental age to avoid causing maladjustment. It is not the nature of the particular activity that makes it appropriate for these transitional students, but how it is run.

What activities should good middle schools have? Following are some programs from middle schools with which I am familiar. Most of them are public schools, and activities may be adjusted by Christian educators. They may serve as an inspiration to a Christian school faculty to develop its own list. Ideas used by schools I have worked with include:

Recreational Sporting Activities
   Tennis
   Bowling
   Badminton
   Gymnastics
   Table tennis
   Hiking
   Individual track and field events
   Bicycle riding
   Team sports—flag football, baseball, basketball, etc.

The above require skill and exercise and could become

lifetime activities. Students can be novices at these activities and enjoy them. Skills will be learned along the way. Much can be done with their attitudes about the sport and most of all about themselves. More activities are:

Crafts—of all kinds

Music Activities
    Band—Priority learning, then performing
    Non-band instruments—piano, organ, accordion, guitars
    Chorus—solo—quartet

General Activities
    Drama—skits—speeches—debates
    Painting—oils—watercolors, etc.
    Travelogue and films
    Reading novels—not in curriculum
    Newspaper reporting and editing
    Cooking and sewing—beyond curriculum
    Computers

The list could be further developed. They should be offered in repeatable short terms of six or at most eight weeks. A record should be kept of what each student takes, and a follow-up conference made to encourage students to expand their horizons. The main purpose of these mini-courses is to increase skills, improve emotional growth and reactions, and to encourage students to choose a variety of challenging and broadening possibilities. As adult leaders in the middle school, think of the development of skills and attitudes that will help them cope later in life.

Teachers are the key to this program's success. Their attitudes toward it determine the students' enthusiasm. Teachers need to believe the mini-course program will be of tremendous value to the students. Just the release of pent-up energy is a side benefit that will show in the regular classrooms. Let me interject right here that even secular schools see the need for offering less sophisticated activities to this age group. No longer are dances given without other alternatives being offered at the same time. In this way a student may wander into a dance for a while and then without embarrassment choose to go to another activity. Remember, these parties are held in the afternoon, not at night. At this age they should be home at night. If they do go out at night, they should be accompanied by mature adults, and not in large, adolescent groups. Night activities should be infrequent and well planned. Adult guidance is needed.

What are some of the skills learned in this program? These vary from course to course. They extend and round out the skills learned in the regular classroom. They are:

Social Skills—Such As To:
Get along with people
Communicate effectively
Give and take in non-controlled situations
Cooperate with others
Persuade others

Emotional/Personal Skills—Such As How To:
Control one's temper
Listen attentively
Handle frustration
Handle success
Avoid being obnoxious
Respond courteously

Mental and Achievement Skills—Such As How To:
Organize the work

Succeed in the project
Complete the project
Use resources—books, films, people

It would take too much space to list all the educational values in this informal process. The intermingling of students in this adult-guided setting, provides students an opportunity to use skills often ignored or not required in the regular classroom setting. No middle school is complete without it. These are the things that teach Christian students to feel comfortable when dealing with others, so that they can witness unashamedly.

Christian schools need to develop their own programs in this area, ones that will encourage commitment, loyalty, poise, reasoning, character, persuasiveness, and other skills that will make the students more effective, for their Lord. What a blessing that would be. The whole Christian community should notice the results. The financial cost is minimal. Students' leisure time will be well spent. More and more, the citizens of today's society are going to have to know how to use their leisure time wisely. They will not learn it well if we ignore it at this delicate age. Middle school students are ripe for learning skills needed to make productive use of their leisure time. There is no substitute for a well-developed and well-run interest area program. Christian schools can develop programs that students enjoy. This is a prime teachable age. Now is the time to get started broadening their interests. It's worth the effort. It will have an effect for a lifetime.

Questions

1. Why was the junior high club program considered inadequate, for the middle school?

2. How did the middle school attempt to remedy the situation?
3. What are some of the personal skills that reinforce those learned in the classroom?
4. Why is this interest area (mini-course) program more appropriate for most students than a rigid club program?
5. What's wrong with high pressure? What do we mean by undue pressure?
6. Why do middle school educators feel that many interscholastic and some intramural programs are damaging to the healthy growth of the early adolescent? What developmental areas are affected and how?

6
Chapel—The Spiritual Hub

The wheel that enables a Christian school to spin smoothly, without wobbling on its hub, is chapel. Chapel serves the purpose of keeping the school on its spiritual track. Chapel includes prayer, praise, Bible reading, and a brief God-inspired message. Every Christian school should have a chapel time. How often? That depends on the circumstances. A regular chapel should be scheduled at least once a week and at additional times as the occasion arises, taking into account student age, the space available, and the resources available.

The content and format of chapel should be carefully planned. It should not be haphazard. Chapel should not be dull routine. It is the most important time in the school day. Unless the student body sees it this way, its usefulness is limited.

Some Christian schools have chapel because it's expected. In those cases it becomes a meaningless form of worship, geared to adults, not middle school students. Chapel should be exclusively times when prayer, praise, Bible reading, and spiritual messages are conveyed. Chapel should model for the students that God is sovereign in all aspects of our lives. He's concerned with everything we do.

Middle school chapel should have varied programs. A staff member should be hired for chapel as for any other area. Like classes in the school, it should consist of high-quality programs with a variety of methods and resources. Any one method bores the middle school child. Interest needs to be high. There should be times of student involvement. They would love to see times of faculty involvement. On rare occasions a sermon will do. But they don't need to be preached at as though they never heard the gospel before. They need inspiration.

We must prepare for chapel like we do for regular subjects in the school day. Like teaching, it should not be "off the cuff." The leadership should be people who "walk the walk." Early adolescents are keen at detecting fakes. Remember chapel exists "to turn them on" to Christianity. Because of chapel they should develop a fresh new outlook on life. If students become "turned off" in school, examine what's happening in chapel. Chapel should do for a school what a pep rally does in an effective sports situation. Pull them together around a cause.

What then is the role of chapel? To operate rightly chapel should:

1. Be a happy place which students value. They look forward to being there. They feel a part of it.
2. Be a place where they receive a spiritual uplift. It's relative to their personal lives. Life oriented.
3. Be involving them, if not in action, in content.
4. Be an exciting place to be. Combination of singing, praying, preaching, drama, testimonies, etc.
5. Be led by preachers, teachers, outside speakers, parents, students, professional athletes, and missionaries.
6. Be carefully creative and well planned.
7. Not be too long. An hour is too much except, for special occasions. Short and sweet.

Christian educators ought to determine what outcomes we want and then use the best ways to achieve them. Never have chapel just because it's expected of a Christian school. Throw your energies into it. Remember, it could produce the opposite effect if not done well. We are not saying "candy coat everything." We are saying, "Give it the best shot you've got."

We want students to love the Lord more because of chapel, and to show their love by the way they live. Just think of the golden opportunity we have to promote Christian ideas and values. It presents us with the opportunity to contradict the world in music, sex, dating, abortion, filthy habits, movies, television, and other abnormal things that the world says are normal. Yes! Chapel is worth the time even if it means extending the school day.

Chapel can be extended to be useful on holidays, whether patriotic or religious. Special events at Thanksgiving, Christmas, Easter, Veteran's day, Valentine's day, Presidents' day, and Memorial day are a few days that could be emphasized. For politically correct reasons, these are neglected holidays in the secular schools, and they often lack dedication and solemnity. Just think of and praise the Lord for how we can emphasize Christian influences as we celebrate these holidays. We are free to give both a patriotic and religious emphasis to these days.

Besides chapel there ought to be school-wide assemblies to conduct debates, have choirs and bands, discuss political issues in which Christians are on both sides, such as the economy, social security, international relations, aging, law and order, and political correctness. Some of these could grow out of regular classroom discussions. Some could include outside speakers. Christian school children ought to be well versed on issues discussed in society. We need not fear worldly influences because we have the last say. Anyway we like to believe that our children are too well versed in their faith to believe falsehoods. They need to learn to intelligently detect false arguments. As educators and parents, we must constantly be vigilant and have confidence in them. A good practice is to invite the parents and general public in, to listen and participate. Good quality programs equal good public relations for the school.

In summary, I believe that chapel is a very important learning time in a Christian school. It is not an add-on but something we must have. Good planning and preparation are absolutely necessary. Goals for chapel should be clearly stated and reviewed occasionally. Chapel helps round out education with content the subject areas may avoid. Christian school students should be knowledgeable on all phases of life. They should be exposed to all types of cultural activities. Remember, we have the last say and can clarify hazy or incorrect thoughts. How better to learn worldly knowledge than under a spirit-led situation? Chapel helps keep the school on its mission.

Questions

1. How frequently should chapel meet? What factors should help determine that frequency?
2. What topics should be discussed in chapel?
3. List a variety of methods that could be used in chapel.
4. What type of chapel programs would you like to have?
5. Why have chapel? What should be the objectives?

7

Tests, Homework, Projects, and the Middle School Concept

The whole school must be consistently devoted to middle school principles. There ought to be unity in what happens in the classroom, and in homework assignments, test administration, in long-term assignments, and in report card preparation. This unity shows that the school truly is striving to meet all of the needs of these unique individuals. It means that the whole school thinks middle school.

Homework:

Children 10 to 14 should not have more than one hour of homework a night, for all subjects combined, except on rare occasions. This is difficult to arrange unless teachers work as a team. Even though they are teaming, teachers "pile it on" at times. Administrators ought to keep tabs on this and control it. Good communications and trust among the teachers are absolutely necessary.

Some schools have different days set aside for different subjects to have homework. For instance, English, Math, and Science may have Mondays and Wednesdays, while Tuesdays and Thursdays are reserved for Social Studies, Reading, and Foreign Language. Fridays are open to any subject. But this is too binding. Flexibility and spontaneity are needed by the teachers. Occasionally going over the hour in total assignments is fine if the limitations of middle school students are respected. The hour is a guideline, not an edict, and it calls attention to the needs of growing children ages ten to fourteen.

Homework should reinforce material that students know already. Untaught material should not be included in homework. Incorrect learning can take place. Then the teacher will have to spend time correcting what was learned incorrectly, which is more difficult than people realize. Review is fine. Further exposure to cement ideas works well. In some general areas, a new assignment is in order. Even in general reading assignments, the teacher should first pull out and review difficult vocabulary words and concepts, prior to expecting the students to read it independently. It helps to clarify difficult ideas in class, too. The teacher can present an interesting challenge to them in their homework reading. This is a fine teaching technique.

The more exacting the material, such as mathematics, the more it needs to be pre-taught in class, lest students learn the material incorrectly. A middle school class must thoroughly understand the material assigned as homework lest they fall into copying, careless mistakes, or just not doing it.

Middle schools need to develop a homework policy. It should be fair and allow exceptions to the time limit for students with special needs at both extremes, advanced and slow. The whole faculty must "buy into it" for it to be successful. Remember not to complicate what is happening to them developmentally by heaping homework on them. Be conscious of the time it takes them, not you, to do the assignment. The homework must be material that has already been taught. We've seen too often that students were not thoroughly taught the material and had too much difficulty with their homework.

They need homework to master what has been taught. Homework also gives the parents an idea of what is being taught. In some subjects, such as social studies and English, new materials are permissible, but difficult concepts, vocabulary, and formulas, must be clearly introduced. It is a good practice to give them "bait" that will cause them to want to do the homework. For example, if they are studying World War II, relate tales of people who were affected by it.

Homework should not be graded. Use check marks (or other accounting) to keep track of whether the homework is being done. A regular overall checking is necessary for this age. Keep parents informed. Be alert and watch for copying.

Have special times for conferences on homework, if necessary. Parents should not be surprised at the end of a marking period by being told homework was not turned in. Students should not be surprised either. They should be well aware of their records.

Wise middle school teachers assign homework lightly. They recognize that homework is a valuable tool in the learning process. They also recognize that there may not be a need to give it every night. It is certainly fine not to give homework every time the class meets. Homework, like daily teaching, should have variety to it, to make it interesting to middle level children.

Keep in mind, that with these students, just because a teacher is "tough" does not mean the students will learn. Conform, yes. They will not be late turning in assignments, but may get help, and learning and understanding may not take place. They are this way, not because they want to be impudent, but because that's where they are developmentally. Hold them to the task. The important thing is that we handle middle school situations with finesse. They have so much to learn about responsible behavior as they grow out of childhood.

Tests

Even in making up tests, teachers need to consider the

educational and physical development of children in transition. Keep the wording understandable, the concepts clear, the length within limits, and the answers short.

1. Final exams or tests covering a long period of time are not appropriate for this developmental age level.
2. Tests should not be intended to trick the student. Techniques to keep the students alert are fine.
3. If they do well, it is a credit to the teachers. Grading a test on the curve is an excuse by the teacher for either poor testing or poor teaching.
4. No single test should make up a majority of a student's grade. Most middle school students can't emotionally handle that. What are you trying to prove? They are so young. Why insist that they be older?
5. Tests are as much a measurement of how successfully the teacher taught the subject, as of how well the students learned it. Be sure we are measuring what we set out to do. We should test in relation to what we taught and the capabilities of the students.
6. A good test for middle school will have a mixture of objective test questions as well as short sentence or brief essay questions.
7. Remember, middle school students have four whole years, high school, to learn further to refine their skills. Keep in mind that middle school is not the end of what is being learned. We want them to leave middle school with an enthusiasm for learning.
8. Keep tests reasonably short, and have tests cover material taught recently. Test frequently, too. Then they can be helped to do better right away.
9. Remember, tests are not given to prove how tough you are. They are given to gauge what students have

learned, and to see what further needs to be retaught or not taught differently next time around.

Assignments

1. The same basic principles apply to assignments and projects. Keep them short and within the skills and capabilities of their age level.
2. Use class time to check up on progress or lack thereof. This should be quick and accurate. Don't take too much class time.
3. Organization is not their strongest point. Show them ways to organize. Continuously and patiently show them ways to organize. Example. Have them keep a notebook with the date, requirements specified, dates different parts are due, and your own time schedule for getting it done. Check it periodically.
4. Don't give long projects, with so many pages. That leads to plagiarism. If you reward length, you will get someone else's work.
5. Encourage originality, creativity, and accuracy. Reward it. Remember, they will get some help from home. Don't discourage it.
6. Encourage multiple resources of good quality, not necessarily quantity. Help them identify quality work. Reward them for it.
7. Keep thinking that your assignments are learning tools, not punishment.
8. Encourage parental help. They are partners in teaching and learning. Encourage honesty as to who did what, and who thought of what. Your honest grading of this will encourage parental cooperation.

That's good for this age level, when they naturally are in the process of rejecting parents.

Middle school students have difficulty keeping tabs of their homework, assignments, and projects. Some teachers suggest that they keep an assignment book to write in daily assignments and other needed data. Chapelgate Christian Academy, in Maryland, requires all middle school students to purchase a special notebook to keep a record of their assignments. Parents are saved from many frustrating nights caused by their middle school children not knowing the homework assignment. Parents like it! The form should have a space for parental comments and signature. This is easy for students to use and for teachers to check. Some students need a great deal of checking while others are more responsible and require very little supervision. The teacher decides that, not the student. Some students respond well to a teacher's challenge, permitting them a limited time to do their work.

I well remember when I was a principal, parents came to me all tied up in knots because their children had no idea what the assignments were. For the students who needed it, we made up a sheet for every teacher to sign each period. Each subject was listed and the student had to write each day's assignment down and get it signed by each teacher. How cumbersome. This homework book made that process unnecessary. The faculty realized they had transitional students who needed help, so they wisely put together this book. It is possible that you may come across with a better idea, if so develop it.

Report Cards

Report cards should be issued frequently, just as assignments. Report cards need clear directions, frequent checking, limited time length, and honest grading. Report cards should be handed out at least every six weeks. Middle school students need to know where they stand. Even though the teacher informs them, it may not register until it's in writing and the parent sees it. Frequent report cards give them the opportunity to improve their work before they get too far behind. Most middle schools follow the traditional nine-week term. Sarasota Middle School in Sarasota, Florida, issues report cards every six weeks. This makes sense, given the nature of transitional children. They respond to frequent evaluation, which results in frequent feedback, and forces something to be done,

A middle school report card should have behavior check marks and room for a brief written statement. Both of these should have complimentary responses as well as needs improvement. A check indicating the need for a parent conference should be there too. Parents need to use this also, to initiate conferences. Don't forget to include attendance and tardiness data. Some will be tardy if permitted. The record of attendance and tardiness reveal a great deal about the student. Yes, reporting is meant to help, not thwart the student.

Brief Summary

This section is meant to convey the importance of considering homework, projects, tests, and report cards, philosophically and in practice, when developing a middle school. It is intended to help the reader realize that these areas, too, must carry out middle school principles. They help make middle school what it is. Remember, all of this is being considered in order to help this age level grow into healthier teenagers. Remember, we have not arrived! As we work with these students, and as society changes, different needs may arise, and we welcome the need for further change.

Neither the children nor us created them, a preadolescent. They were created in God's image, which became tarnished by sin, and we daily see the result. May we who are involved with middle school students not foul up HIS marvelous creation. Let us as a school present opportunities for them to accept the Savior, and assume the further responsibility of creating a school environment that will discipline them. Again I say, "What an awesome responsibility."

Questions

1. Why is it important to bother about the length of projects, type of homework, or frequency of reporting periods?
2. What is wrong with long projects? Why not work them hard?
3. Why don't we give a high school type of report card? "They have to grow up someday."
4. What does human growth have to do with remembering their assignments, or anything else for that matter?
5. Why is it necessary to consider the growth and development of middle school students in the areas discussed in this chapter?

8
Scheduling in a Middle School

What is the recommended division of the school day and week? Why not use the self-contained day that was so common in the elementary school? How about the six-period day of many high schools? Well, it doesn't matter which division you make for middle level, as long as there are frequent breaks for rest and relaxation. Middle school youngsters need a planned change of pace quite often. Teachers with long class periods often abuse the time allotted. Sometimes they teach for a little while and make the rest of the period a study hall. This is fine occasionally but not daily. Other times they lecture all period. This is a very poor method if done exclusively. So middle school teachers thrive on shorter periods with variety built into them. Middle school students, naturally, have a short attention span. If teachers don't hold their attention, some of the students will take center stage. What then can administrators do? Punish the students or teachers? Can they be a help to the teachers' dilemma?

The key thing to consider is the division of time that leads itself to the best learning environment for middle schools. Schools have historically experimented with a variety of time divisions. Most of them were pretty sound. What caused their failure? Well, eventually administrators and teachers lost the vision for what brought about the change, and the time schedule lost its purpose. The same could happen to the middle school concept, if we once lose sight of why we advocate these things.

Historically, the traditional six- or seven-period day existed in most schools, middle and high. That seemed to be the easiest way to accommodate the wide number of different courses taught today. In the usual high school, this worked well. It had popular public support because it is similar to the high school parents attended. Some problems existed in the high schools with the required number of hours for science labs, by accrediting associations. So in some cases, double periods were required. This broke up the nice blocks of periods that allowed for all of the elective courses to be taken. Individual students had to make adjustments, which often meant sacrificing desired courses.

Today, some high schools have instituted two or three hour block periods on certain days. The schools can offer more subjects this way and have much less hall traffic. Some schools like this. High schools have their own reasons for doing what they do. But what about the middle school?

The history of the junior high is more relevant here. Initially the six-period day was common. This institution, which so avidly aped the high school, actually became a miniature high school. It imitated all programs of the high school, the scheduling, the teaching method, and even the extracurricular program. It wasn't long before junior high educators became disillusioned and looked for other ways to schedule. What they inherited from the high school was not suitable for this younger student body. Some of them moved to block scheduling and in some cases team teaching. Natural combinations for scheduling purposes were English (Language Arts) and Social Studies, and then Mathematics and Science. Students were block-timed according to when they had these subjects. Remember, the adolescent ninth-grader was in the junior high at that time. Their presence meant that the junior high schedule had to meet the Carnegie Unit regulations for time spent on a subject. This posed a real problem, as mentioned before, in science. The use of block time worked better with team teaching, but there were too many flaws in trying to developmentally meet the needs of such a wide range of students. At least it cut down on what junior high students do so poorly: change classes. In many cases the bell said to them, "on the mark, get set! GO!" And go they did!

Along came another attempt to make an adequate schedule. The Junior High Core Curriculum, which accommodated the double period very well. It used thematic units that were sensitive to the students' growth level. It stressed social and personal development. Many of the units were practical, dealing with problems of daily living. It attempted to relate subject matter to life and to give it more meaning than a topic far removed from their daily lives. It was rightfully assumed that if a subject was important to the learner, the student would learn more readily. Some of its efforts were poorly done and much of it was discarded. The best elements of block time, team teaching, less hall traffic survived into future programs.

Back to scheduling, some schools, even middle schools, tried an A day and a B day. There were a multitude of courses being suggested, without time limits. It did enable schools to offer a wide variety of enrichment courses. This was further an attempt to make good use of faculty resources and to cut student hall movement during the day. This was similar to the new ideas mentioned above, of block-timing the day. Some junior highs and middle schools still use a form of it.

The jury is still out. Each method is used and works well in some schools and not in others. The competence of the staff and faculty affect even the best plan devised. As an experienced administrator, I am convinced when teachers are effective, the schedule is effective. I do believe that given the same set of circumstances, a better schedule can enhance the teaching process. Also, with middle school students, consideration needs to be given to their growth patterns even when designing the schedule.

Administrators have many unbending variables when constructing a schedule, and sometimes these overrule growth considerations. First, the administrator must think in terms of how many faculty members there are, their specialties, their competence, what age level they relate best to, and optimizing class sizes. These things are important in setting up a smooth-running school.

Second, the administrator must consider the constraints of the building. The location and size of labs, shops, foreign language labs, library, gymnasium, computer room, home arts room, lunch room, art room, drama room, music and band rooms, guidance offices, and halls. Noisy activities need to be separated from those that demand quiet. Much confusion can be avoided by locating classes intelligently.

Third, thought has to be given to the effect that student development has on their ability to handle noise, movement, and other distractions. Before assigning a room, you must consider the need for electrical outlets. It is wise to also track a few groups to see how far they have to go from class to class. Scheduling is a very complicated process.

Given the above considerations, what then is the schedule being recommended by this experienced administrator, who has been through most of these schedules? Only in advanced, non–middle school courses, which carry high school credit, is there a time limit per period. This is due to the requirements of the Carnegie Unit, which must be earned to graduate from high school. There is plenty of time in high school to earn those units, and only a small percentage of students are ready for them during middle school. The good middle school administrator accommodates these courses without permitting them to dictate the rest of the schedule. An alert and aware administrator can do this. Don't permit these advanced, non–middle school courses to have priority, or the schedule tail will end up wagging the whole academic dog.

Middle school administrators need flexibility to take care of the varied needs of their student bodies. We also know that these transitional students must be attended to when setting up the schedule. Their attention span is short. Because of the rapid growth changes taking place in most of them, they can't sit still for long. Too much is happening in their growing bodies. They also bore easily. They need frequent lavatory breaks. They can't control their behavior enough to be "let loose" without supervision. It is important to find a schedule that prevents many of these adjustment problems from becoming serious.

But is this solely a scheduling problem? It is not! It is a problem of scheduling and teacher competency. On many a school observation visit, the principal would showcase the most competent teacher and expect me to believe that the whole school was the same. Of course, in that teacher's classes, there were no discipline problems and the high quality of work was exciting. Parents too were pleased and proud of what was being done. They knew good teaching was taking place by the reactions and statements of their children at home.

Teachers, given an amount of time in the schedule, use it well if they are middle school advocates who recognize the children's growth needs. They allow for a carefully supervised break, constantly aware of what could happen if the class is unorganized for these unorganized students.

Some teachers need help in doing this, and it is the administrator's responsibility to provide such help. Some teachers may need to learn how to develop good lesson plans, how to organize their class materials and accompanying methods. The instructionally educated administrator is a must. In addition, he must know how to work well with teachers. Administrators also must see to it that all subjects are receiving quality attention. Sometimes in block timing and team teaching, this is not the case. Good communications between the administration and teachers makes a quality school. There should be no guessing game on either side. Their honesty with each other is of prime importance. The administration supplies the schedule and has the responsibility to see that the teachers use it wisely.

The administrator's task is to provide opportunities for teachers to understand the middle level child. The act of teaching is a continuous in-service program, much of which is arranged by the administrator. This need not mean more meetings for already busy teachers. They can be a part of the team teaching planning process, which the teachers themselves lead. Resource people, books, films, and videos should be made available to them too. The meetings should deal with live problems that teachers meet every day and why that particular team has those problems. It could involve individual problems, team problems, and total school problems. It also could consist of teachers helping teachers, but without judging them.

Sample middle school schedules follow. Each one contains something meritorious, but may not be good for any one particular school. Be creative when constructing middle school schedules. Provide ample time for schedule planning. Learn from your mistakes. Don't repeat them the following year. Listen to what your teachers have to say. Continually develop an inventory of ideas from your faculty. Take a problem inventory. Share what you are developing with your faculty, if possible, but don't bore them with details. Remember the final decision is the administrator's to make. It can't be "put off" on somebody else.

Always keep the public informed. They sincerely want the children to have the best education. Don't let them rely on rumors or rely on a guessing game about what is happening at school. A well-informed public will be your staunchest support.

Schedules:

1. A public school schedule has many of the elements recommended in this chapter. Their publication says, "What makes a good schedule?"
"The schedule provides the following (edited by author):

Interdisciplinary team planning
Departmental team planning
Adequate time for lunch
Mini-courses
Flexibility
Allows for school within a school"

This middle school schedule has blocks of interdisciplinary time. It also accommodates disciplinary team planning time. In a middle school, both should be emphasized. Think of the advantages of specialization when needed, and the possibility of discourse between teachers of different disciplines. One is more accommodating to subject content, and the other to transitional children's growth needs. Both need to be accommodated in a middle school. The approximately 42-minute periods are not too long, provided that teaching methods are not mainly lecture. More importantly, I say again for emphasis, it accommodates a team of teachers who have the same children, and gives the teachers the opportunity to decide what individual students need help and how to help them. It further enables the team to help a group of students who need special attention. Think of how useful this guidance function would be. It can be done!
2. A suggestion by the principal of another school further supports what is recommended for middle schools. He calls it, "The Pod/Interdisciplinary Schedule." This schedule calls for interdisciplinary teams, composed of English/Reading/Social

Studies for each of the three grades in the school. In this school some three-subject interdisciplinary teams meet in the morning, while other three-member teams meet in the afternoon. With their staff and the space available, this school had only three subjects on the team in the open pod. These three teachers meet a set of children in common. They have planning time together to discuss academic problems, work habits, curriculum changes needed, grouping changes needed, and general school-wide adjustment. The team may decide different groupings are needed for specific reasons, and may make changes without a lot of red tape.

This ability of teams to make important decisions is crucial to the success of the teams. It is one of the strengths of team teaching. Imagine the same group of three teachers with the same group of students, for three periods. It's another form of the old self-contained class. The difference is that in content and developmental adjustment we now have the expertise of three teachers rather than one teacher. At least that is the thought of many educators today. The complexity of content in most courses today, even on the middle school level, is more than one teacher can handle.

This type of schedule enables the interdisciplinary team to specialize in content when needed, to group/regroup, to split time as needed, and even to plan whole group meetings of the students when advisable. In other schools, the interdisciplinary team may well consist of a different set of subjects. The enthusiasm of the faculty is a must.

Some teacher personalities find it difficult to work on teams. Much in-service training is needed for them. Some should not be in teams. A good administrator can work this out to the benefit of the students as well as of that particular teacher, especially if that teacher is highly respected.

There is no doubt that the interdisciplinary team serves an excellent guidance function. This is one of its strengths. The closer to instruction the guidance function becomes, the more effective it will be in routine daily situations. Often the team is setting up the situation to which the students are reacting. This is not an attempt to dismiss the value of a well-trained guidance counselor. The counselor will work with teaching teams in large groups of students and with individual students and parents. Then there is the standardized testing program to administer. This is explained in another chapter.

There is no one way to set up a middle school schedule. Determine the peculiar needs of the early adolescent, then work within the limitations of the staff and building facility, and work out a schedule that best takes care of these students' needs. Do what you and your staff believe to be right, considering all issues.

When working on schedules, work on givens first. Those subjects that only meet one period, or those in which a teacher can only come in at a certain hour, etc. In many Christian schools, this is a reality. Then place teachers in situations where they will most likely succeed. Notice movement. Do the students have to go far from one class to the next? Include teachers' input before major decisions. They may have valuable suggestions. In your schedule, if you expect teams to function well, they will need to be provided common planning time. Don't skip that. Arrange a time during which part-timers can meet with the teams, at least briefly.

This is a problem in private schools. Some of their best teachers can give only a few hours of teaching a day. Work out ways in which they can easily communicate with the team. Have faith in your teachers. Give them every support you can. Surprise them with goodies to show how much you appreciate them. Should a team of teachers or an individual teacher have any difficulty, let them know of your availability. Either help them or find someone who can. When you are seen as a partner and not a threat, the school will be a happy one.

Principals who spend time in the office putting out fires should wonder why they have so many disturbances. Are they overlooking staff situations that need correcting? Do the teachers take them seriously? Does a clique of teachers make the decisions for the principal? Do parents have too much say? Are private matters kept private? Is there backbiting?

Good principals must know more than how to make a schedule. They see themselves as the educational leaders of teachers. They are true teachers and respected as such. They must keep the total staff aware of the needs of transitional children and what is best for them. If they do, they will be on their way to having a successful middle school. Principals with good schedules show the insight needed to do all that is necessary to have an effective school. They will feel good when they hear, "Well done, thou good and faithful servant." The schedule is the beginning of a successful school experience. Take it seriously. It is your responsibility to work out a good and effective schedule to the glory of God, for it is Him we serve, not man.

Questions

1. What things does a middle school administrator need to consider when making a middle school schedule?
2. How long should middle school periods be? Explain.
3. What do we mean when we say, work on "givens" first?
4. If your school is too small for team teaching, what do you want the teachers to be sure of?
5. Where does guidance fit into a schedule? Explain.

9
The CEO-Administrator

The early adolescent requires an administrator who models Christian behavior as taught in the Scriptures, and who also is decisive, consistent, caring, fun, knowledgeable, mature, mentally healthy, fair-minded, and understanding of the early adolescent. The administrator also needs to be a leader of teachers, an interpreter to parents, and dedicated to students of this age. No one individual can possibly possess all of these qualities. But the administrator can strive for them. Let us say, "This age level needs an administrator who has it all together, because the student doesn't."

A crucial step is discernment when hiring so that the staff is appropriate. When you don't have the opportunity to hire your own staff, your task becomes that much more difficult and a faculty in-service program needs to be developed.

A good administrator seeks a teacher who:

Establishes and encourages a good school and classroom atmosphere.

Desires to be with this age-level.

Is competent to teach in at least two content subjects.

Enjoys being with children throughout the day. Lunchroom and playground, before and after school, activities, and other free time.

Works well with the administrator. Cooperative, honest, and supportive.

Is organized. Likes things done in an orderly fashion.

Has a firm but fair and kind discipline.

Has an orderly but fair grading system. (The teacher must submit to the administrator for approval, before using.)

Keeps parents well informed. (Sees them as partners, not adversaries.)

Is willing to sponsor an interest area (club).

Is willing to perform duties.

Above all, is a committed born-again Christian.

With a faculty that has the above mind-set, the school is bound to produce effective Christians. But more is required of an effective Christian administrator.

A good administrator is:

Responsible for the curriculum. This is especially important in a Christian school. In other words, what really is covered in class.

A teacher of teachers. Supervises and instructs teachers in topics such as:

Use of audio-visuals (appropriateness or lack of).

Use of bulletin boards.

General appearance of the room.

Classroom discipline.

Discussion techniques.

Interest of students (blasé, lively, stimulating).

Preparation of teacher for that lesson.

Making adequate lesson plans.

Keeping attendance and tardiness.

Keeping an orderly grade book.

Encouraging professionalism within the staff.

Reinforcing the above increases the professionalism within the school.

The administrator must know what to look for and how to improve it. Teachers too must know what is a priority with this particular administrator. They need to recognize the administrator's observations as an attempt to help them.

A good administrator is also concerned about students. Some people call this administrivia, but it is very important in a well- run school.

Students should have:

Adequate places to hang coats and store books.
Adequate time to change classes, eat, go to lavatory, etc.
Proper clothing.
Adequate rest.
Good work habits.
Good health.
Good mannerly hall behavior.
Ethical classroom behavior.
Good lunch etiquette.
Good relationships with teachers and peers.
Materials necessary for learning.

Schools exist for the students, and professionals should do all that they can, to provide a safe, hassle-free environment so that maximum learning can take place. The school administrator has the responsibility to see that this is the case.

The general condition of the school rests with the administrator. If something goes wrong, the administrator needs to act on it, promptly. No excuses! This may mean confronting a faculty member or even a parent. This never is a pleasant task. It is hardball all of the way and is a part of being an administrator. Such is leadership. When things are successful the administrator gets accolades.

Parents are always a concern of administrators. Some are very difficult. Some have weight in the church or community and make sure you know it. The necessity of being a good diplomat who can handle delicate situations successfully is primary. This, coupled with a good prayer life and dependence on the Lord, is vitally important. Most parents will be a blessing to the administrator, even praying for whatever is needed.

A good administrator:

Works well with parents and shows them courtesy.

Interprets the school to them. Parents need to be familiar with the policies, curriculum, methods, etc.

Provides for parent volunteers. If possible, it is nice to set aside a special room. Do something to tell them how much they are appreciated. Never has volunteers sit idly by and do nothing. They then start thinking negatively about the school and feel unneeded.

Plans assemblies, chapel, and cultural events.

Works with civic groups for the benefit of the school. Community service: a Christian school must be seen by the public as a testimony for the Lord.

Checks lavatories and other physical facilities, to see the general condition of the school. This tells you something about the student body and administration.

Visits classrooms frequently. This can be for a few minutes or for a whole class period, depending on the purpose and what's happening in that class at that time. Such supervisory visits should not be predictable to students or teachers. Yet some visits may be mutually planned for specific reasons.

Evaluates teachers. Teachers should know the administrator's goals for them. The process should be to assure teachers, thus giving them a sense of security. A good evaluation process improves instruction.

The administrator does these things in a non-threatening way. In a healthy situation, teachers take it that way.

Further, effective administration requires keeping up to date on professional developments. There is much that the Christian administrator can learn from secular literature and professionals. It then can be Christianized. We are not sponges. We know how to discern and use what we can.

Therefore a good administrator:

Is a recognized part of the system who works well with the school board, pastor, elders, and others.

Recognizes that administering requires good teamwork. Contributions of others are valued. But the final authority rests with the administrator.

Evaluates the latest educational developments for the school and plans their implementation.

Promotes the school in newspapers, magazines, television conferences, etc.

Makes necessary changes without equivocation.

The various duties of an administrator are endless and sometimes thankless. When I was first appointed principal, a secular person in the business world said to me, "Remember, the nearer to the top you go, the lonelier it will be." That has not always been the case. There were many rewarding moments, but there will be those second-guessers who question your decisions mercilessly. The effective administrator can and does sift this out and has peace even in situations like this. Prayer helps, too. Any leader will have his/her critics. We choose how it affects us. Be confident and strong in the Lord. Always pray with and for your adversaries. In order to be successful, an administrator has to resolve how to handle unfair criticism in a

God-inspired manner. Then it won't cause you to make an unwise decision.

Administration cannot be counted by hours. A lot depends on the nature of the individual. Can he/she delegate? Some people can't. Can he/she trust? Does he/she have "rabbit ears?"(negative baseball term) meaning hearing criticism. Does he/she respond well to stressful situations? Does he/she protect teachers from unreasonable demands? Does he/she know how to end telephone conversations and conferences? A person considering entering administration should answer these questions honestly. No one has "arrived," but these points need to be understood. Remember, a happy administrator equals a happy effective school. The reverse is true also. An unhappy administrator equals an unhappy staff and student body, and an ineffective school. Administrators are not made of iron, but are instead a combination of bendable gold, diamond hardness, and iron, to form a priceless alloy.

A middle school administrator can have a high-quality and effective school if the above suggestions are heeded. It must be consistent with the administrator's beliefs, personality, character, and leadership style. No two administrators have the same mix of these ingredients. Some are more authoritarian, nervous, temperamental, or introverted, while others are more group-oriented, understanding, flexible, and sharing authority. Some are disorganized and inconsistent. No single way is proper for everyone. It's what works that counts. Ask yourself, "How do I operate most effectively?" Then be sure that some of the faculty takes care of your shortcomings. Don't fake it. It won't work. You have a lifetime of idiosyncrasies to correct. Experience will refine you.

As I've said before, there is much to be learned from secular schools. The following secular school has an exemplary program. The Mayfield Woods Middle School in Howard County, Maryland, has a complete list of goals, some of which are mentioned below. As you read them, think of what goals you need to develop for your Christian school.

A Public Middle School Goals (edited)

- To keep in view of staff that the primary mission of the school is to enhance student achievement.
- To see that systematic plans are developed to upgrade student proficiency in basic skills.
- To be sure that students are given clear, written and verbal directions: key points of instructions are repeated: and student understanding is checked.
- To assist in creating a positive learning environment within the school.
- To protect learning from disruption.
- To share and delegate responsibilities so that teachers have input in school decisions.
- To make sure appropriate sources are available.
- To promote staff development to enhance teacher skills.
- To delegate responsibility and spend more time with instruction-related activities.
- To see that discipline is clear, firm, and consistently enforced.
- To ensure that students, staff, and parents, know the rules and periodically review them.
- To see that school facilities are kept clean and reasonably attractive.
- To see that interruptions are avoided, general announcements are limited to non-instructional time (before and after school).
- Transition time between classes and activities is minimized.

- Class time is structured so that teachers stay on task.
- Student pull-outs are minimized.
- To insure that there are opportunities for parent involvement and that they are communicated to the community.
- To make sure that success by students and staff are recognized.

These give a good indication of some of the responsibilities of an administrator. Besides the normal, they contain a concern about class interruptions by the intercom system, class interference by pull-outs, and the need for recognition of students and staff when warranted. Notice the extent of the duties. Even if two administrators were to perform the exact same duties, the results would be different. No one is a carbon copy of another. The list may be similar, but the person carrying it out is different. That makes a difference.

In my experience of working with administrators, I found that there were wide differences in the methods, philosophy, personality, and temperament of the principals. I didn't try to make them a carbon copy of me. As long as what they were doing didn't violate what was best for middle schoolers, I was satisfied. Suggestions were made for improvement, but it would have been wrong to expect intelligent professionals to mimic me. Yet you will find some administrators who work that way. It is the goal that counts, and the principals were being reached from a variety of directions. I kept nurturing them and encouraging them, just as I wanted them to do with teachers. The big question was: "Did they continue to develop middle schools principles, when I, the Director, retired?" They did and still do. They were able to stand on their own two feet. They learned well and believed what they learned.

The administrator who is secure is on a firm foundation that what is being done is best for this age level. Middle schools need the very best administrators assigned to them. In large systems they must not become the "dumping ground" for people unsuccessful at the other levels. In Christian schools they are needed to promote and implement a special level of education that is in danger of being overlooked. That would be a tragedy. Someone knowledgeable about the needs of early adolescents is mandatory.

In closing, middle school administrators need to remember that their students were not all at the same level emotionally, spiritually, physically, or academically. Isn't that a wonderful challenge? Some are just beginning to unfold developmentally, and will catch up to some of those who up to now, always were ahead of them. The more successful your administration is, the more diverse the students will be. We don't exist to make them all the same. Our job is to keep working with them even when they appear to be disinterested. Be an encourager, a confidant. The adult who is influential with students at this age is truly affecting a lifetime. This is a very teachable age. They are reading adult models (without being allowed by peers to show it), sometimes accurately and sometimes inaccurately. Quite often there will be a delayed reaction and you will hear years later what an effect you had. They learn by your example, not by your words.

If it is fairness, persistence, cheerfulness, confidence, and self-respect that you want your students to develop, then let them see these characteristics in you and your staff. A good administrator is interested in the students and staff, and lets them see it. Keep in mind that no school is without problems. When problems become normal and students crowd the office, the administrator had better get a hold on the problems. The key person is the administrator. who causes the motor to run smoothly or to sputter. The buck stops at the administrator's door. In spite of all of this, it is an extremely rewarding experience, one that will have eternal value. It is a service of joy!

Questions

1. What are some of the characteristics a Christian administrator should possess? What do you think are the three most important of these?
2. In selecting teachers, what criteria does an administrator need to use? Why is this one of the administrator's most important duties?
3. In setting up the school, what student needs should be considered?
4. Compare your goals with those of a public middle school. Note what is similar, dissimilar, and what needs to be changed.
5. Summarize what you think shows a successful administrator.
6. List the ways in which Christian administrators are the same and are different from their secular counterparts.
7. What safeguards should a principal formulate when recruiting and assigning parent volunteers?

10
Report Cards—How Am I Doing?

In a middle school, report cards mean more than the students' grades. When dealing with early adolescent students, much more than intellectual achievement must be considered. This should be accomplished in a non-threatening and gentle way in a middle school through the use of conferences, scheduled at least twice a school year. Here the subjective items can be presented. Such things as work habits, manners, ethics, cooperation, health, growth problems, relation to other students, teachers, administrator, and other adults, are very important for the children and their parents to know. Many of them are unrecognizably different at school than at home. These things help determine what students do with what they learn. Traditionally, society gives little or no attention to these areas. Most parents want to know what grade the student makes in each subject.

I say include conferences in the grading process, but don't make them equal in importance to the letter grades. Just say, "Here is some further information you may want." Make it voluntary. Tell them how it is important in helping children grow. Let them know that what you put in writing in these areas, at this age, will not be kept at the end of the school year. If misbehavior that affects learning persists, only then can the record be summarized and passed on to the next level. Things that happen as children mature should not forever "bug" them. Recognize that children, at this age, are changeable and that as a school, they will be helped to make positive changes. Be sure the parents understand that by working jointly with the school, they can be assured that their children receive help.

Teachers will need training in presenting positive information, and in using tact when negative comments are presented. In these days of lawsuits, teachers need to know how to collect data, how to present it, and how to avoid opinionated ideas. It is not easy. Teachers need rules for their own protection, even in Christian schools. Every conference should have a written summary, jointly composed by parents and teachers, and signed by both. Parents sign that they have seen it and are free to comment on what they've seen. Notice that both parties, teachers and parents, are working together. The written report should say where they differ.

These conference evaluations tell much about students and what they are doing or not doing with their capabilities. These public shools recognize how important it is for parents and teachers of children this age to be in close communication. "We encourage communications between home and school and welcome sharing information and strategies with you." Mount View parents can arrange to have conferences with individual teachers, a team of teachers, or both. They go on to say that, "Student evaluation is an ongoing process. At any time a parent conference can be arranged." Parents would do well to have as much knowledge of their children at school as they can acquire.

The basic report card is different and serves a different purpose. What do parents expect of report cards? What do parents want to know? What do parents need report cards to tell them? Parents want to know how students are performing in their subjects. The report card should indicate how well students know the material being taught. Are they making normal progress? This can be done with overall grades that in general show how they perform. The report card should be simple to read and understand. It should not be cluttered with a lot of trivia. A school that needs to make a decision about students should rely on all information in their records, not solely on report cards. There should be room for clarifying statements, such as, "Jon is doing his work daily, but he could be better prepared for tests." "Melanie seldom has her homework done." "David is easily distracted in class." "James is a conscientious student and does more than the required work."

Parents should be told what particular needs and strengths their children possess. Consequently, parents or teachers may call for a conference. There should be documented data on the report card to support comments. More will be said about the report card later. Now to continue with conferences.

Teachers as professionals should control the flow of the conference. There should be an agenda. If students are going to be discussed, they should be on call, near the conference. At some time they should be brought in on a summary, and their agreement or disagreement should be noted. Courtesy and respect should be exhibited by all parties. These conferences are usually called when either parents or teachers are not satisfied with the progress of students. They should be called for favorable things too, not just the negative ones. The point of these conferences is, how can we help students do better now? These conferences can be in addition to the regularly scheduled conferences, which are a part of the reporting process.

In some cases the parent or teacher cannot wait for a scheduled conference and needs to deal with immediate concerns. Conferences are intended to help parents help their children.

But it doesn't always work that way. It's been my experience that some teachers appear to the parent to be vengeful and dominant: "My way or else take the consequences." They are

93

the authority figure and complete submission by the parent and student is expected.

True, the teacher should be in control of the conference and not let it get out of hand, nor let it become a shouting match. As the professional, the teacher should possess some dignity and guidance skills. It is the teacher's responsibility to establish a fair and comfortable climate. If unfair comments are made by the parent, keep cool, and maintain a professional attitude. Don't lower yourself to the level of the comment. Don't be sarcastic! Be calm and be firm. Stick to the problem at hand. In fact, terminate the conference when accusations start flying: then politely schedule another conference, this time with a third party present, preferably the principal. It is wise for the parent to know that an administrator or some other third party will be present. Some parents are so biased for their children that they won't be able to work satisfactorily with any teacher. However, this is not an excuse for the teacher to be arbitrary and unreasonable.

In a Christian school, the administrator can say, "It may be best to withdraw your child from school." The administrator is the moderator and must make sure the teacher or parent is not being unfair. Sometimes even teachers and parents of Christian schools are unreasonable and unfair. That's why prayer is advisable before, during, and after a conference. Set a positive tone. However, such difficult conferences are the exception. The average report card conference or spontaneously called conference is pleasant, even when the child's progress is poor. Most parents recognize the need for help when working with this developmental age. They know that these students are "experts" at dividing and conquering the adults in their lives. When differences especially with parents do arise, it is advisable for the teacher to keep the principal well informed. Otherwise the parent may tell the principal only one side of the story, which is the truth as the parent sees it. An effective principal hears both sides before taking action.

The above are my recommendations. The professional needs to gather more data than is on a report card for the scheduled reporting conferences. Copies of the work done are useful and also enlightening to some parents. Also useful are data about behavioral characteristics, such as frequent tardiness, little or no homework, test grades, attitude toward teacher and subject, and typical excuses. Positive comments on these matters would be very fruitful.

Good teachers realize they are teaching live human beings. The children are not just a bundle of impersonal subject content. Such teachers will want the students to love the subjects they teach, and this benefits their relationships to the students and parents. If students respect the teachers, they will respect even the difficult subjects they teach. The teacher needs to be alert and sympathetic to the student. A true professional knows that students don't leave all of their "garbage" at the classroom door. Good teachers, especially Christian teachers, will be sensitive to the students, who need help with life's problems.

Students this age need some other significant adult, besides their parents, to help them overcome what to them are overwhelming problems. They don't appreciate the "prodding" teacher. But listen to students, and they will reveal much. Be ready to be a friend in need. This doesn't diminish your respect or authority. Strangely enough, it increases it. The key is whether you lower yourself to be a member of their peer group, or truly become a significant adult who understands.

What grading practices are common for report cards today? One is the traditional A, B, C, D, E, or F. This well-understood system rates a child in relation to a grade level standard. The A, B, C, D, E, or F system has served the school well for generations. It attempts to set a standard of measurement which parents like and understand.

Then there is an attempt to give students a grade in relation to their ability. This seemingly humane idea didn't tell the parent what students achieved in relation to a group standard. It was without standards. Parents did not like that. In some cases this ability-level system resulted in teachers giving high grades to students who have not met the minimum achievements. A student could conceivably receive an A and not be able to do the work, if the student was working up to maximum ability. This leaves parents with no common scale upon which to measure their children's progress. All they knew was the children were working up to what parents felt was a mythical ability.

Some schools give parents a grading system that incorporates both ability and achievement. In such situations the school feels that the parent needs to know a student's capacity to learn at that period in life, as well as the degree of content mastery in relation to commonly accepted norms, as measured by a standardized test (IQ). Caution is advised here. Students perform erratically on tests. They may score less on a standardized IQ or achievement measurement than they should. Also, many early adolescents will believe they can't do any better, and give up. Growth spurts also take place. It would be wrong to say you can only perform this well, and we don't expect more. Many students will try to work up to the teacher's expectations. Use standardized tests as guidelines, not edicts. Also, children with the same IQ tests (ability) have different work habits and attitudes. I've seen many students who performed much beyond their measured ability.

This is not as big a problem in a selective Christian school as it is for its public counterpart, because the ability range is not so wide. There are students in Christian schools who do not do well even when they score well on standardized tests. Teachers need to ask themselves, are the students doing the best that they can? Do we as a Christian school have the professional expertise to know what to do with this type of student? What do they need to do better? It may be something as simple as lack of sleep, a loving teacher, or careless work habits. Maybe the type of instruction used is not communicating to the early adolescent. It could be that there is disruption at home.

There are a number of things to look into when thinking of what to report to parents, either by conference or built into the report card. Honesty is the best policy.

There is another important area that needs mentioning. The middle school should take the responsibility to inform parents of the extent to which students have mastered the basics, the famous three "R's." What specific skills has the child truly mastered? These can be worded in objective form. "The student can write complex sentences." "The student can recite the presidents of the United States." "The student can multiply fractions." "The student can write a paragraph with its proper parts." "The student is able to spell grade-level words." "The student can read for details." In this way the parents may be assured that their children possess the expectations of their grade and more. These make knowledge more valued by the students, and help them function well in academics.

Middle school teachers should include mastery of the basics in their teaching. In every subject, at this grade level, the basics must be emphasized. Middle school is the last chance that students will be able to learn the basics by teachers trained to do so. Think of how important it is for mastery to take place. These basics are the tools of the trade. Science and Social Studies (History) require students to write and communicate, just as fluently and effectively as English or Reading. All teachers ought to expect literate papers. The effective middle school report card contains a report of the basics in that subject, as well as a grade of the content.

There are other areas for which middle schools are responsible that often are not formally evaluated. These personal skills are important in that they help determine the human qualities that make the students effective with the vast knowledge they have learned. They help make the difference between the truly educated person and the regurgitator. Too often, learning is regurgitation.

The problem is that parents, and the public in general, do not value the teaching of these personal skills. They are subtle. The Christian school should make an effort to teach them, and be conscious of the curriculum subjects where they can best be taught. Be cognizant of the school's effectiveness in communicating these skills. Make them a priority. Where would such things as self-confidence, poise, reasoning, manners, dexterity, caring, thoughtfulness, kindness, organization, stick-to-it-iveness, etc. be consciously taught? What good is a person who is an empty shell, with only knowledge, and no feeling of personal worth in order to share with others? Where is the servanthood advocated by Christ nourished?

This is a challenge. We need to develop a systematic way of identifying and reporting these skills. This is where the Christian school can excel in developing a product that is uniquely Christian, something that parents notice. It is a good faculty project, especially in a Christian school, to work these into each subject area. A good principle to follow when encouraging this is, if the staff doesn't "buy into it," it is doomed for failure, and the students will be the losers. We challenge you to measure the product. What difference does attending a Christian school make? It is the quality of the person that counts. At no time is the parental responsibility in this area abrogated. The primary responsibility is theirs, but the school can assist.

Going back to report cards once more, how often should grades be issued in middle school? Knowing the age level and their short attention span, the authors believe that they should be given in less than the traditional nine-week reporting period. We would advocate every six weeks. This is consistent with the problems related to the growth level of the children. It is frequent enough to be within their memory. It will help keep them on task. They won't drop too far behind so that it becomes impossible to improve.

Sarasota Middle School, in Florida, has this unique reporting procedure. They understand that the early adolescent needs it. Parents benefit because they can keep better tabs on their children. With the arrival of the computer, this problem may not exist. It soon may be possible for parents to have daily access to current grades in every subject every day. It's possible. Sounds like an administrators and teachers nightmare, doesn't it? The same will be true about conferencing. Just think of all the possibilities.

In closing, a school should not make it impossible for a student to obtain a decent grade. Be fair. Middle school students stop trying if they find that no matter how hard they try, they do no better. Think in terms of what goals need to be reached, and what is the best way to get there? A good working relationship between parents, teachers, and students pays high dividends. But after a short time of frustration, the students will tell the adults "to bug off." Work with them properly in middle school, and they will be honored to have adults in their lives in high school.

Many ways of reporting are being recommended in our schools today. Study each one. Be sure your school's parents are informed of impending changes. Show them how much more they will know about their children because you make this change. Parents will feel more comfortable with a grading system similar to the ones they had in school. Keep in mind the purpose—to let the parents know how their children are doing in school. Most of them have a good idea. They just want that idea confirmed. The reporting system is meant to help students improve, not to tell on them. The students become better pupils because we reported the right information. That is our aim.

Questions

1. Why are conferences especially important for the early adolescent? Along with the subject matter grade, what other information is important to present?
2. Why is it advisable to have frequent (every six weeks) reporting periods?
3. How will we report the students' accomplishments objectively, in the basic skills?
4. In a Christian school, why is behavior important?
5. Why are conferences necessary, at this age?
6. How can a school staff measure personal skills?
7. What is the purpose of report cards in a middle school?

11

Parents: Whose Children Are They Anyway?

Parents should be knowledgeable of school practices.

There was a time when Christian parents had complete confidence in the public schools. Whatever they said was right, and the student suffered the consequences unquestioningly. Not any more. Parents are disillusioned and suspicious. Societal changes have seriously affected the schools. Many ideas, both educational and political, the school is required to support are alien to a majority of the general public. In trying to accommodate a diverse group of students from the handicapped to the gifted, from the law-abiding to the violent, and from many ethical and cultural backgrounds, it seems that none is satisfied. Instead of taking care of particular needs of a specific group, they merely homogenized the goals.

I'm not saying ignore the needs of these precious children, but I am saying take care of their needs properly. Christian parents are concerned about what comes across to them as an anti-Christian secular bias. This is why the public, which pays the bills, must be alert and active in their schools. Parents can make a difference! It further illustrates a need for school boards and administrators to work with their public as partners. The general public demands to know their schools' policies. They have that right! The parents' understanding depends on the openness of the administrator. They have made noble attempts to keep a disinterested public informed. But without the public realizing it, school boards and administrators knuckled under to special interest groups and changed the values the school could support. Thus the public schools found themselves out of harmony with large segments of their supporters.

No matter how hard the disillusioned parents tried, their pleas seemed to fall on deaf ears. Interpretation of laws, even by the Supreme Court, affected what the schools could do. In many cases schools were helpless. In the Bible Belt, schools in many districts taught Bible as a course, while in other areas they could celebrated Christmas. Bible reading and the Lord's Prayer opened up the school day. In recent times society and the schools seemed to forget whose children they were dealing with, anyway. In the change the Christian basis of American society was ignored. No longer could America's beloved public schools even remotely honor the beliefs of the overwhelming majority of the people. The Judeo-Christian ethic no longer predominated. Consequently, newly formed Christian schools burst on the education scene.

These Christian schools would do well to remember they exist because of the dedicated desires of devoted parents and therefore, avoid anything that takes them away from their purpose. May these new founded schools remember to whom the students belong, parents who want their children taught in the Judeo-Christian ethic. These Christian parents, with limited funds, desire that their schools will be the best institutions of learning. They want good schools! They want their children to be able to vie with the best the public schools have to offer. Christian educators, be careful that you don't alienate your public. Remember the reason for the Christian schools' existence, and that won't happen. Parents will support you unflinchingly, if the school stays consistent with what the sacrificing parents want them to accomplish. Respect them! Remember whose children they are anyway.

What type of knowledge do parents need of these new schools? They need everything that will build up their confidence in the school. They want to know how discipline is conducted, school dress code, test scores, academic programs, regulations, transportation, teacher certification and qualifications, school certification, field trip policy, grading policy, illness and absences, lunch room menus and services, chapel (how frequent and what topics), and anything else they may question. They like to feel that their children are not receiving a secular education nor an inferior curriculum, which is not worth the time and money invested.

It must be remembered that most parents are not professional educators and can misinterpret data when it is presented to a novice group in an unorganized way. Make your presentations clear and avoid jargon. Keep confidential data confidential. There are confidential things that only those involved should know. Assure parents of the confidentiality of such information, such as whether or not the child has received psychological counselling, or a child's intelligence quotient, or family difficulties. Some things must remain in confidence. There are things that even school personnel need not know about students, parents, or each other. The administrator should keep in mind that there are some things that are private and personal. There will be teachers and parents with only partial information who will make judgments about an individual or situation that has no justification, but the administrator is bound by confidentiality, and not bound to explain such rumors. A good policy to follow is that personnel matters should remain private. Never discuss a personnel matter with an uninvolved parent or student, no matter how close they are to you personally. It is so tempting to justify your own actions. But teachers, parents, and students have the right to have their personal business kept private. A competent administrator always respects that right. Remember the title of this chapter. Whose children are they anyway? However, all of this does not detract from the need to have the information available necessary to a student's success.

Two areas are important for parents to know: (1) the general policies of the school and (2) their child in particular. I'll repeat them with apologies for being redundant. They are that important.

(1) The Policies of the School in General

The personnel is professional.
There are adequate materials.
Policies are reasonable.
The school encourages suggestions.
Discipline is fair and consistent.
Academics are solid.
Basics are taught.
Teachers are fairly accessible.
Parents are welcome.
Scriptural principles are emphasized.
School is orderly and safe.
Grading is reasonable and under control.
Expectations of each classroom.
Acceptable dress code.
The quality of students.
Professionals are born again believers.

The parent is a valuable partner in a good school. Administrators and faculty should not look on parents suspiciously. Nor should they cast aspersions on them. This cancer should be nipped in the bud. The better you are at communicating the school to them, the more supportive they will be. Do not leave room for them to suspect that you are holding back information that they should know. Don't make them rely on the unofficial pipeline.

(2) Their Child in Particular

Adjustment to school (classes, other children, teachers).
Test scores. Interpret them.
Academic progress or lack of it.
Ability to do the work.
Attitude about others.
Behavior.
Work habits.

Don't discuss individual teachers with them. Be supportive of the teachers. Whenever a parent comes in and the discussion centers on a teacher, make an appointment for a joint conference, if the parent pushes the point. Steer the meeting away from getting emotional. The goal of the administrator is to be an arbiter. It is to maintain the dignity of the conference, to move it away from personal accusations, toward working out a solution. Sometimes there is no solution. Perhaps suggesting a change of teacher or adjustment in subject is necessary.

The parent may need to learn from the conference, too. Direct the parents. In a Christian school, you can always advise them that they may withdraw their child if the child refuses to react in a Christian manner. You have a responsibility to the other students to keep control. Keep in mind it is your show, and you are in charge. Remember, communication is a two-way street, and the troublesome parent needs to be reminded of that. Parents appreciate a positive administrator. Also remember that the actions of some teachers can't be justified under any circumstances. Yet even that is not a public issue, but a private one between you and the teacher. Assure the parent that you will check the situation. Parent conferences with the administrator are usually very rewarding and pleasant. It is up to you to bring out the best in parents.

Parent volunteers are a help in the smooth operation of schools. Any school can make good use of parent volunteers. These are becoming more and more scarce as mothers become increasingly employed. These parents feel a joint responsibility with the school to help educate their children. How can parents help? This varies from school to school. In general, parents can help by:

Working in the media center.
Being classroom aides.
Assisting in the office.
Volunteering for the workroom.
Helping in the health room.
Assisting teachers in the lunch area.
Chaperoning on field trips, etc.
Supporting school fund-raisers.
Working in parent-teacher groups.
Working with outside community agencies.

These point out how vital parents are in the smooth running of a school. Trust is needed by both school personnel and parents. There will be some teachers who do not want parent volunteers. That's fine, too. Some don't know how to use them well. If the parent volunteers feel included in the school, they will become the best public relations experts possible, and good workers too! An effective administrator realizes this and works diligently with parents. If the administrator does, it makes the running of the school easier.

Parents want school personnel to be honest, straightforward, open, creditable, and courteous. This whole chapter on what parents want is based on the fact that they first want trust. And they want to know that their children are in good hands. They want to believe that this school, created for Christian families, has their best interest as their goal. Also, they will respect you more if they know you have set the parameters and that they need to work within those limits. Parents take pride in knowing that there are limits that protect the students' environment and also the teacher's right to privacy. Parent volunteers in the building help if they see the rules applied consistently. Inconsistency in the handling of students and even parents breeds dissension.

Like all teams, schools need an arbitrary leader, and as administrator, you are it, difficult as that may be. A good piece of advice: be professional at all times, even in the most trying times. Don't go on the defensive. A good offense is better than a confused defense, which gets personal. If you get too defensive, parents will wonder what you are hiding? Always document your conferences. This is necessary, especially in this day of litigation even in Christian schools.

An administrator who can admit an error to teachers, students, or parents and then do what is necessary to correct it is a rare gem. Parents want administrators who know good manners and use them. They appreciate one who has the faculty under control. Staff backbiting, feuds, dissension, and lack of administrative respect means a troubled school. Isolated staff members who do these things don't mean the whole school is troubled. But the problems must not be ignored and left to fester. They won't go away.

If you get a flood of parental complaints, look into your own leadership style and the faculty reaction to it. Change some of your ways and change personnel when needed. The buck stops with you! Parents, like faculty and students, are not the decision makers. They give input, but you make the decisions.

If the decisions take parental input into consideration, then harmony will result.

What do parents really want? They want a well-run school in which their children will learn in a safe, intellectual, harmonious and spiritual atmosphere. They look to the administrator as the professional who puts all things together. Don't waffle. Parents expect an administrator to be a decisive person of faith, good character, and strength. Parents want to know whether or not their school is Christian in faith and practice. They want to be aware of suggested changes and their consequences. They want to feel there is an appeal process. Whose children are they anyway? Remember that in a Christian school the school still acts "in loco parentis." Consequently, parents of the school must be supportive of the school's beliefs. The school must remember the children belong to the parents.

Questions

1. Summarize the types of events that caused parents to become disillusioned with the public schools.
2. Why is it important for administrators to maintain confidentiality? What are topics that should be kept in confidence?
3. Pick the three most important items that parents need to know about the school and about the child.
4. In what ways can parents be of help to the school? Be specific. What should not be available to them?
5. What is meant by the statement: "You as the administrator need an arbitrator, and you are it"? How important is it?
6. Why bother working with parents anyway? Either they like it or they don't! After all, the Christian school is a private school. Justify its importance.

12

Evaluation of a Christian Middle School (Instrument For)

Christian educators involved in middle school education need an instrument that measures how close it is to middle school principles. This instrument is designed to reveal the strengths and weaknesses of an existing middle school. It does not cover every vital area, but the instrument has validity and will assist in the development of an in-service program. It will keep the faculty focused on middle school principles, instead of the biases suggested by non-oriented middle school teachers and parents. How true to middle school principles is your school? This instrument was initially developed by a group of middle school principals and teachers, and was altered for Christian schools by the authors.

Directions:

Place the number that indicates the degree to which your middle school meets each of the criteria below. One (1) is low, and (5) is high. A total of 160 is very good, while 110 is fair, and 75 to 110 means needs improvement. Anything less than 75 needs serious study and is very poor. This instrument and its scoring was developed after thirty years of experience with middle schools.

Our middle school's spiritual quality:

1. The total staff, principal, secretaries, custodians, and volunteers, model Christian behavior. _____
2. The faculty conducts class in a decent and orderly manner, using a firm but kind discipline._____
3. Whenever warranted, the faculty prays with students and parents. _____
4. The faculty responds to crises in a Christlike manner (no sarcasm, belittling, ridicule, temper, etc.). _____
5. The faculty stresses Christian principles in the content being taught. _____
6. The faculty seeks to stress the positive, in the learning process. _____
7. The faculty exhibits an understanding of early adolescent behavior. _____
8. The faculty encourages parent conferences before a crisis exists. _____
9. The faculty has fair grading practices. _____
10. The total professional staff consists of born again believers. _____
    TOTAL
    _____
    _____

Our middle school teaching methods:

1. Promote a comfortable classroom climate, where all children feel accepted. _____
2. Acknowledge that even in a private Christian school, children are at different learning levels, and adjust the learning process and expectations accordingly. _____
3. Include group guidance when recognizing common classroom problems. _____

4. Work with students by using methods that help them assume responsibility for their own learning. _____

5. Use a variety of teaching methods (small groups, lecture, oral reports, recitation, projects). _____

6. Use individual conferences with students, without embarrassing them (teachable moment). _____

7. Instruct students in developing good study habits. _____

8. Provide a clear, fair evaluation, based on the developmental level (i.e., No single test or project should determine most of a grade). _____

9. Accept that students need to have time designated for talking and moving around. _____

10. Include the teaching of responsibility, respect, organization, manners, ethics, and values when teaching content. _____
    TOTAL _____
    _____

A Christian middle school curriculum:

1. Enhances the total student's personal development (spiritually, physically, mentally, socially). _____

2. Provides for the development of spiritual values and biblical supporting knowledge. _____

3. Refers to the Bible in all disciplines. _____

4. Provides opportunities for all students in the Related Arts areas (art, physical education, home arts, music, computers, shops). _____

5. Provides opportunities for growth in student decision making (in class and elsewhere). _____

6. Provides experiential content from life, needed to improve society. _____

7. Diagnoses, then teaches the need of each student in the basic skills. _____
8. Incorporates the most up to date technology. (Science, computers, visual aids, machinery, etc.) _____
9. Provides for cultural enrichment and performance in the Arts. _____
10. Provides advanced studies when warranted. (The opportunity is there for the gifted.) _____
TOTAL _____
_____

Our middle school's educational environment:

1. Provides each student with a healthy, challenging environment, free from undue pressure or harassment. _____
2. Provides, under adult leadership, for peer group interaction and values discernment (carefully guided leadership). _____
3. Provides for controlled interaction with peers, in a non-classroom situation. _____
4. Encourages healthy, ethical interaction with adults (teachers, parents, volunteers, staff). _____
5. Provides opportunity for self-contemplation by having a quiet time, to themselves. _____
TOTAL _____
_____

Our middle school staff members:

1. Show by their teaching and decisions, that they are knowledgeable of early adolescent growth patterns. _____
2. Are knowledgeable in more than one subject. _____
3. Are well adjusted and emotionally healthy. _____

4. Exhibit a preference for middle school students
   by the way they react to students.   _____
5. In addition to teaching content, they function as
   counselors and spiritual advisors.   _____
6. Work cooperatively with the administrator.   _____
7. Relate courteously and intelligently with parents._____
8. Willingly accept extra duties assigned to them. _____
   TOTAL   _____
                                                _____
   GRAND TOTAL   _____
                                                _____

This is not intended to be a scientific instrument, but it should give a good indication of whether or not your middle school has those ingredients recognized as peculiar to middle school. How close is your school to the ideal, and where is the need? Feel free to improve on the instrument, and develop your own. This would be an excellent faculty exercise.

What do you think is important to measure? Why is it necessary to evaluate a middle school? What is the end product of your middle school? Did you make a difference in the children? Are they better children because they attended your school rather than another? The authors would welcome any suggestions you may have. Send them in. Let us know your scores so that we can improve the instrument.

A Creed

The teacher of a middle school should be willing to subscribe to the following beliefs. They are essentials in order for the school to be an effective one. These beliefs are good reminders of what we are all about. They focus attention on the task. Let me remind you that Christian students go through these developmental stages too. That cannot be avoided, but it can be eased by proper handling.

The Middle School Creed the Staff Believes

The staff believes that there is a need for a school specifically designed for the early adolescent because:

The early adolescent is in a variable, fast-growing developmental period.
All children do not grow at the same rate.
Physically and in each other area they do not grow at the same pace. Therefore, it is possible to have a physically mature emotional pygmy, and vice versa.
This growth change requires a teacher with a healthy mental hygiene and a deep academic background.
A caring, settled, firm, flexible, lively environment, controlled by professional adults, is needed.

The staff further believes that middle school teachers should be caring, competent, academically superior professionals, knowledgeable about this developmental age level.

The staff believes that middle school students should be free from undue pressure and inappropriate competition. The implications are as follows:

No highly organized interscholastic activities.
No final exams. Grades should not depend on one big test or project. Frequent grading periods work best with this age.
No sophisticated adult-type social activities. The more informal the better.

The staff believes that this developmental age level is a

period of life when peer groups are of primary importance and the instructional strategies should capitalize on this.

The staff believes that a general education program consisting of the academic areas, related arts areas, computers, and physical education be required of all students in each of the three years of middle school.

The staff believes that except for high-school-credit courses some exceptional students may take, middle school courses are freely offered at any number of hours needed. This allows for the needed flexibility.

The staff believes that early adolescence is a good time to emphasize values. The staff should identify which values to emphasize (honesty, acceptance, tolerance, respect, persistence, consistence).

The staff believes that this is a good time to expand horizons. A good mini-course program is warranted (interest areas, clubs, hobbies, intramural programs, field trips and other enrichment opportunities).

The staff believes that middle school teachers need to be creative and interesting, with multiple methods.

The staff believes that it has the responsibility to continually develop programs for this ever-changing age group. What a challenge! We must never act as though we have arrived. There is always need for justifiable change.

The staff believes that middle schools ought to be significantly different from elementary or high schools because the students are different. They are in the formative transitional stage, which needs adult culturing and guidance, but not dominance.

The staff believes that administrators in middle school ought to exert a firm, consistent, but kind discipline.

In summary, the staff must believe they can make a difference in the lives of early adolescents. If they do, they will be more prepared for what is ahead.